HORACE
IN HIS
ODES

INTRODUCTION • TEXT • NOTES • VOCABULARY

BY

J.A. HARRISON

Formerly Senior Classics Master,
Methodist College, Belfast

Published by
BRISTOL CLASSICAL PRESS (U.K.)
General Editor: John H. Betts
and
BOLCHAZY-CARDUCCI PUBLISHERS (U.S.A.)
(by arrangement with Bell & Hyman, Ltd.)
1988

Cover illustration: Horace, detail from the *Ara Pietatis Augustae*
of Claudian date; Villa Medici, Rome.

Printed in the United States of America

First published 1981
Reprinted, with corrections, 1985 & 1988

U.K.
BRISTOL CLASSICAL PRESS
226 North Street
Bedminster
Bristol BS3 1JD
ISBN 0-906515-57-2

U.S.A.
BOLCHAZY-CARDUCCI
PUBLISHERS
1000 Brown Street, Unit 101
Wauconda, IL 60084
ISBN 0-86516-062-7

CONTENTS

LIST OF ILLUSTRATIONS

FOREWORD

This book introduces the reader to some of the best of Horace's odes, bringing together 33 from the total of 103.

The selection is not arranged after the order of the poems as they appear in our texts. That order was probably chosen by the poet himself. The first 9 poems in Book I are all in different metres, as though to demonstrate the poet's range of metrical skill. The only arrangement by subject is in the first 6 poems of Book III – the so-called 'Roman' odes. Elsewhere dedicatory, humorous and philosophical odes are mixed together, making it more difficult than it always is to tell whether Horace is serious or jesting and whether the ideas expressed are his own or are assumed for the purposes of a particular poem.

The arrangement adopted in this volume is intended to give an insight into the personality of the poet and, by showing different aspects of his work, to illustrate his outlook on life. The poems selected are divided into 5 sections:

I.   Religion, Philosophy and the Shortness of Life
II.   Friends
III. Love
IV.   Countryside
V.   The Roman State

The division is a rough one, for Horace can include many topics within a single poem: for example, *Odes* III 8 (Poem 16 in this volume) within its 28 lines refers to religion, friendship and affairs of state; and also contains that touch of humour which pervades much of Horace's work and which sometimes goes unnoticed unless attention is drawn to it.

Indeed, the personality of Horace has an unfailing appeal. We may admire Virgil, we never feel we know him. We all believe we know Horace. However, the 'Horace' one person imagines may differ widely from the picture formed in someone else's mind. Most people agree that he was an extrovert, that he liked his fellow-men and that he enjoyed life to the full. It is when we come to a more detailed assessment that opinions differ. This is what one would expect. We may know our neighbour well and feel that we rather like him or dislike him, but we cannot delve into his heart and analyse his motives. How much more difficult it is to form a rounded picture of Horace from his writings. This book will certainly not provide sufficient evidence, but the poems will, it is hoped, make the reader interested in Horace and lead him to read further in his works. For that purpose a programme of further reading is given on p. 112. Some secondary bibliography is also given there but in general this volume makes no attempt to collate and comment on the many scholarly works written on the subject of Horace.

The general introduction is designed to provide the barest essentials on Horace's life, works and the metres he uses. There is also a short introduction to each of the five sections; *the views expressed there are meant to provoke discussion, not to expect agreement.*

The text of each poem is accompanied by three things: a short appreciation, notes and a short alphabetical vocabulary, containing only unusual words or words with some special meaning in their context.

This book is intended for readers of all ages who have reached the necessary stage in their Latin studies. In practice it may be used most often in the two post-'O' Level years. For I am convinced that some Horace should have been read by all 'A' Level Latin candidates.

I wish to acknowledge the help given me by the Bristol Classical Press and their Reader in the preparation of this book. I received ideas also from two main sources: L. P. Wilkinson's *Horace and His Lyric Poetry* and, for poems from *Odes* III, from G. Williams' excellent commentary on that book. Thanks are also due to Professor McGann of the Queen's University, Belfast for his advice on several points. J. W. D. Semple, Head of Classics at Campbell College, Belfast, read the whole manuscript, corrected some errors and made many useful suggestions. Illustrations are by Jean Bees and Patrick Harrison.

Port Erin   J.A.H.
May, 1981

POEMS INCLUDED

Poem	Odes	Odes	Poem
1	I 10	I 3	14
2	I 21	I 5	20
3	III 6	I 9	9
4	I 34	I 10	1
5	III 2	I 11	10
6	II 3	I 21	2
7	II 10	I 22	8
8	I 22	I 23	19
9	I 9	I 24	15
10	I 11	I 25	22
11	IV 7	I 34	4
12	II 14	I 37	29
13	III 30	II 3	6
14	I 3	II 6	27
15	I 24	II 7	18
16	III 8	II 10	7
17	III 21	II 14	12
18	II 7	III 2	5
19	I 23	III 5	30
20	I 5	III 6	3
21	III 9	III 8	16
22	I 25	III 9	21
23	III 26	III 13	28
24	IV 1	III 14	31
25	III 18	III 18	25
26	III 25	III 21	(17)
27	II 6	III 25	26
28	III 13	III 26	23
29	I 37	III 30	13
30	III 5	IV 1	24
31	III 14	IV 5	32
32	IV 5	IV 7	11
33	IV 15	IV 15	33

INTRODUCTION

I. Life of Horace

The essential facts are these. Horace was born on 8th December, 65 B.C. in Venusia in the south of Italy. His father was a freedman who saved enough money as a tax-collector to give his son a first-class education, a thing for which Horace expresses great gratitude. After attending the best teachers in Rome, supervised by his father who showed him what to imitate and what to avoid in the big city, Horace went on to Athens to read philosophy. While there he was swept up in the civil war first between Brutus and Cassius and then perhaps between Octavian and Antony. He fought on the republican side as a military tribune at the battle of Philippi (42 B.C.) with little distinction. He returned to Italy under an amnesty and, finding his farm at Venusia confiscated, managed to exist on a minor post in the Treasury. The turning point came when Virgil and Varius recognised his poetic talent and, in 39 B.C., introduced him to Maecenas, Augustus' 'Minister of Culture'. From then to his death in 8 B.C. Horace was a member of the literary set that gathered around Maecenas and, especially in his later years, became a close friend of Augustus himself.

II. The Works of Horace

In Hexameters: *Satires* (35 – 30 B.C.)
                           Epistles (20 – 13 B.C.)
                           Ars Poetica (ca. 20 B.C.)

Lyric Poems: *Epodes* (ca. 30 B.C.)
                 Odes I – III (23 B.C.)
                 Carmen Saeculare (17 B.C.)
                 Odes IV (13 B.C.)

III. The Metres of the *Odes*

The music of Horace's Odes is one of their great charms. The reader should learn the rhythm of the various metres so that he or she can read the Latin, preferably aloud, and hear the music. The metrical schemes below should be referred to as soon as a new poem is started. It is also a good idea to memorise the stanzas and lines quoted below.

The probable division into feet for each type of line is shown first. The Latin examples which follow show only length of syllables and caesurae. The symbols – = long syllable, ∪ = short syllable and || = caesura are used throughout. The last syllable of each line is shown as long though a short is also permitted there.

(A) ALCAIC named after the early Greek poet Alcaeus of Lesbos.

    lines 1-2   – | – ∪ – – | – ∪ ∪ – | ∪ –
    line 3   – | – ∪ – – | – ∪ – –
    line 4   – ∪ ∪ | – ∪ ∪ | – ∪ – –

Example: nūnc ēst bĭbēndūm, || nūnc pĕdĕ lībĕrō
            pūlsāndă tēllūs, || nūnc sălĭărĭbŭs
            ōrnārĕ pūlvīnār dĕōrūm
            tēmpŭs ĕrāt dăpĭbŭs, sŏdālēs

(B) SAPPHIC named after the early Greek poetess Sappho of Lesbos.

    lines 1-3   – ∪ – – | – ∪ ∪ – | ∪ – –
    line 4   – ∪ ∪ | – – –

Example: rēctĭŭs vīvēs,||Lĭcĭnī, nĕque āltūm
            sēmpĕr ūrgēndō||nĕquĕ, dūm prŏcēllās
            cāutŭs hŏrrēscīs||nĭmĭŭm prĕmēndō
               lĭtŭs ĭnīquūm

(C) ASCLEPIAD SYSTEMS named after the Hellenistic poet Asclepiades of Samos.

Four types of line are used in different combinations:

1 *Lesser Asclepiad:*
    – – | – ∪ ∪ – | – ∪ ∪ – |∪ –

2 *Pherecratean:*
    – – | – ∪ ∪ – | –

3 *Glyconic:*
    – – | – ∪ ∪ – |∪ –

4 *Greater Asclepiad:*
    – – | – ∪ ∪ – | – ∪ ∪ – | – ∪ ∪ – |∪ –

SYSTEM 1 uses only Lesser Asclepiads: for an example see Poem 13 (III 30) below.

SYSTEM 2 consists of alternating Glyconic and Lesser Asclepiad:

Example: dōnēc grātŭs ĕrām tĭbī
            nēc quīsquām pŏtĭōr||brācchĭă cāndĭdāe

SYSTEM 3 has 3 Lesser Asclepiads followed by a Glyconic:

Example: dīvīs ōrtĕ bŏnīs,||ōptĭmĕ Rōmŭlāe
            cūstōs gēntĭs, ăbēs||iām nĭmĭŭm dĭū;
            mātūrūm rĕdĭtūm||pōllĭcĭtŭs pătrūm
               sānctō cōncĭlĭō, rĕdī.

SYSTEM 4 uses 2 Lesser Asclepiads followed by a Pherecratean and a Glyconic:

Example: sīmplēx mūndĭtĭīs?||hēu quŏtĭēs fĭdēm
            mūtātōsquĕ dĕōs||flēbĭt ĕt āspĕră
              nīgrīs āēquŏră vēntīs
                ēmīrābĭtŭr īnsŏlēns.

SYSTEM 5 uses only the Greater Asclepiad:

Example:
tū nē quāesĭĕrīs|| – scirĕ nĕfās|| – quēm mĭhĭ, quēm tĭbī

(D) HEXAMETER + ARCHILOCHIUS MINOR
(– ∪ ∪| – ∪ ∪| –) named after the early Greek poet
Archilochus of Paros.

Example: dīffūgērĕ nĭvēs,||rĕdĕunt iām grāmĭnă cāmpīs
    ārbŏrĭbūsquĕ cŏmaē

SECTION I

Religion, Philosophy and Shortness of Life

If being religious means believing in one's gods, in the efficacy of prayer and sacrifice to them and in the stories concerning them, then Horace, like most educated men of his day, was not religious. The fact that his writings are full of references to Jupiter and the other gods does not mean that he believed in them. The Olympian family, their attributes and biographies were part of literary convention, just as writers may refer to biblical characters and incidents without being themselves Christian. Also, it was felt by the Roman ruling class that the common people should be encouraged in their superstitious belief in the anger and help of the gods. This would make them more amenable to direction from above and would help to curb their passions. Therefore state religious observances were carefully maintained and supported by writers. Ovid expresses this policy succinctly when he writes: *expedit esse deos et, ut expedit, esse putemus.*

If Horace is unlikely to have believed in the gods of Olympus, it is even less probable that he took seriously the idea of the divinity of the emperor Augustus. This idea was useful politically, especially in the eastern provinces. But could Horace take as a god a man with whom he became more and more friendly and who used to tease him about putting on so much weight?

Educated Romans looked to philosophy, not to Olympus, for guidance. Some followed the stern doctrines of the Stoics who taught that virtue was to live in harmony with reason, to be indifferent to good or bad fortune, and to pursue absolutes like bravery, justice and continence. Others favoured Epicureanism based on the theory that all things are accidental, caused by the coming together and dispersal of constantly falling atoms; at death all feeling ceases, so in life one should follow the senses and avoid disturbing entanglements; the highest good is the absence of pain. Horace is anything but consistent in his religious and philosophical speculations. In religion he is an agnostic rather than an atheist, for he does at times feel that there may be a divine power that guides our lives; see Poem 4 (I 34) below. He can discuss philosophy seriously up to a point but he then stands back to laugh at too much pompous theorising. The 'virtuous man' of the Stoics, he says, is second only to Jove, rich, free, king of kings, sane – except when he has a nasty cold in the head! As an Epicurean, he can describe himself as 'a sleek little pig from Epicurus' flock'!

One theme that comes out clearly and repeatedly is a belief in the Aristotelian Golden Mean, the "nothing too much" preached at Apollo's temple at Delphi; see Poems 6 and 7 (II 3 and II 10) below. This and the inevitability of death were the nearest Horace ever got to a fixed personal creed.

As for death, the ancients thought about it as little as possible. They were mainly concerned with this life. But nevertheless almost everyone, except convinced Epicureans, believed in some sort of survival after death. It could be the dead living on in the tomb and fed by offerings or the Homeric idea of a chill, cheerless Hades or the favoured heroes who went to Elysium or the Isles of the Blest. Of the philosophers, Plato undertook to give a rational basis for immortality. Aristotle said that only the intellect survived. Epicurus denied any survival; some Stoics believed in survival for the wise, others denied it.

Mystery religions usually promised immortality for their initiates but judgement and punishment for the wicked. Pythagoreans preached the transmigration of souls but Horace laughs at this in *Odes* I 28.

Poems 9 to 13 below show that Horace inclined to Epicurus' view. The only thing that survives death and which can give a sort of immortality is fame. There is a limit to what can be said about enjoying life while it lasts and about the certainty of death. Horace repeats himself occasionally in these poems, but such is his musical and verbal artistry that the re-statement of a theme is not felt as a boring repetition but as something fresh and beautiful in itself.

POEM 1 (I 10)
(Sapphic)

Mercuri, facunde nepos Atlantis,
qui feros cultus hominum recentum
voce formasti catus et decorae
    more palaestrae,

5   te canam, magni Iovis et deorum
nuntium curvaeque lyrae parentem,
callidum quidquid placuit iocoso
    condere furto.

      te, boves olim nisi reddidisses
10   per dolum amotas, puerum minaci
voce dum terret, viduus pharetra
    risit Apollo.

      quin et Atridas duce te superbos
Ilio dives Priamus relicto
15   Thessalosque ignes et iniqua Troiae
    castra fefellit.

      tu pias laetis animas reponis
sedibus virgaque levem coerces
aurea turbam, superis deorum
20   gratus et imis.

    This poem is in the form of a hymn to Mercury. He was an Italian god of trade and commerce but, on being identified with Hermes, took over the Greek god's manifold functions. Horace here runs through some of them: skilled in speech; president of the games; messenger; skilled in music; the Thief; helper; of the golden Wand; conductor of souls.

    The poem has the lightness that suits a youthful, mischievous god: see *catus* (line 3) crafty, sly; *iocoso furto* (lines 7-8); the change from *minaci voce* (lines 10-11) to *risit Apollo* (line 12)—the great god just couldn't keep a straight face! There is no religious feeling in the poem.

The ode is based on one by the Greek poet Alcaeus. It may have been meant to be sung, though Horace's poems would usually have been read aloud by the poet before an invited audience.

notes

1. facunde, as god of eloquence. **nepos Atlantis,** his mother was Maia, daughter of Atlas. **3. voce . . . palaestrae,** the mind was trained by oratory, the body by exercise. **catus,** can be 'intelligent' or 'crafty'; the latter is more likely here. **4. more,** 'by the regular use (of)'.

6. nuntium, he was herald of Jupiter and the other gods. **parentem,** 'inventor of'; he scooped out a tortoise-shell and put strings across it to form the first lyre, later using it as a gift to placate Apollo. **7. callidum,** *with infinitive* 'clever at . . .'. **8. furto,** while still an infant he stole the cattle of Apollo.

9. te, governed by *risit,* line 12. **10. per dolum,** he drugged the dogs watching the herd. **puerum,** with *te,* 'still an infant'. **11. viduus ·pharetra,** the boy even stole Apollo's bow and quiver. **12. quin et . . . fefellit,** Mercury guided Priam to the Greek camp to recover the body of his son, Hector, killed by Achilles.

14. dives, he was carrying a rich ransom. **15. Thessalos,** Achilles came from Thessaly in Northern Greece. **Troiae,** dative.

17. tu, note how the hymn is bound together by *Mercuri* (line 1), *te* (lines 5 and 9), *duce te* (line 13), *tu* (line 17). **laetis . . . sedibus,** the Elysian fields. **18. virga,** the magic wand (*caduceus*) given to Mercury by Apollo. **levem,** the spirits of the dead are a *turba levis*. **coerces,** in the way that a dog rounds up sheep. **19. superis deorum,** to the gods of Olympus. **imis,** to the gods of the Underworld.

vocabulary

anima (1) *soul*
Atlas, -antis (m.) *Atlas*
Atrīda (l.m.) *son of Atreus*
bōs, bovis (f.) *cow*
catus (adj.) *crafty*
coērceo (2) *to keep together*
condo, -ere *to hide*
cultus, -ūs (4) *way of living*
decōrus (adj.) *graceful*
Īlium (n.) *Troy*
īmus (adj.) *lowest*
inīquus (adj.) *hostile*

iocōsus (adj.) *sportive*
levis, -e (adj.) *unsubstantial*
pius (adj.) *good, righteous*
quīn et *nay even*
quisquis, quidquid *whoever, whatever*
recens, -entis (adj.) *newly-created*
repōno, -ere *to place*
rīdeo, -ēre, rīsi *to laugh (at)*
sēdes, -is (f.) *dwelling*
superus (adj.) *higher, upper*
viduus (+ abl.) *deprived of*

to be sung by a chorus of youths
28 BCE - dedication of Apollo temple
on Palatine?

POEM 2 (I 21)
(Asclepiad System 4)

gods

a cult trinity

Dianam tenerae dicite virgines,
intonsum, pueri, dicite Cynthium   *mountain in Delos*
    Latonamque supremo
        dilectam penitus Iovi.

dicite eam

Diana's attributes
places

5   vos laetam fluviis et nemorum coma,
    quaecumque aut gelido prominet Algido,
        nigris aut Erymanthi
            silvis aut viridis Cragi;

Apollo places
attributes

Apollinem

    vos Tempe totidem tollite laudibus
10   natalemque, mares, Delon Apollinis
        insignemque pharetra
            fraternaque umerum lyra.
                    acc respect

god & Augustus

hic bellum lacrimosum, hic miseram   *chiasmus*
                [famem
    pestemque a populo et principe   *alliteration*
                [Caesare in
15   Persas atque Britannos
        vestra motus aget prece.

Like Poem 1, this is a formal ode. It is addressed to the twins
Diana and Apollo with a reference to Apollo's power to dispel
war and pestilence. It may have been sung by a mixed chorus at
the dedication of the Temple of Apollo on the Palatine Hill in 28
B.C. in honour of the victory of Octavian (Augustus) over
Antony and Cleopatra at Actium. Apollo, Augustus' favourite
deity, had a temple at Actium which Augustus restored after the
battle. The ode (especially lines 13-16) may also be inspired by
the formal closing of the Temple of Janus to indicate that peace
reigned throughout the Roman world. It is not clear why Diana is
included; perhaps the temple featured a sculptured group of
Apollo and Diana together.

The tight construction of the poem should be noted: Diana
(line 1), Apollo (line 2), Latona and Jupiter (lines 3-4), attributes
of Diana (line 5), places sacred to Diana (lines 6-8), places sacred

to Apollo (lines 9-10), attributes of Apollo (lines 11-12), Apollo and Augustus (lines 13-16).

notes

2. intonsum, Apollo is a youthful god and Greek youths wore their hair long. **Cynthium**, Apollo is called *Cynthius* from Mt. Cynthus in Delos where he and Diana (Cynthia) were born. **3. Latonam**, Latona, Greek Leto, bore Diana and Apollo to Jupiter. **4. dilectam**, *diligo*, 'to love' should be distinguished from *deligo*, 'to choose'. **Iovi**, dative for *a* (*ab*) with ablative after perfect passive is common.
5. vos, = *virgines*; supply *dicite eam*. Diana was an open-air goddess of forests and streams. **6. prominet**, 'is prominent', 'stands out'. **Algido**, Mt. Algidus in Latium. **7-8.** Erymanthus is in Arcadia, Cragus in Lycia; so Diana ranges from Italy through Greece to Asia Minor.
9. Tempe (Greek neuter plural), when Apollo slew the dragon Python to take over the shrine at Delphi, he went into temporary exile at Tempe in Northern Greece. **10. Delon**, Greek accusative of *Delos*. **natalem Delon Apollinis**, 'Delos the birthplace of Apollo'. **11.** supply *Apollinem* with *insignem*. **12.** **fraterna**, 'given by his brother', see Poem 1 (I 10) line 6 note. **umerum**, accusative of respect 'as to his shoulder': translate 'on his shoulder'. Apollo shouldered his quiver when angry, his lyre when in calmer mood. Some take *umerum* as a further object of *tollite* with *insignem* agreeing.
13-16. in this stanza note the chiasmus (*bellum lacrimosum . . . miseram famem*) and the strong alliteration (*pestem, populo, principe, Persas*) common in prayers. **14. principe**, 'Princeps' was the title Augustus liked best; it probably stands for *princeps civitatis*, 'first citizen', a term applied to Pompey by Cicero. **15. Persas atque Britannos**, *i.e.* as far away as possible, to east or west; the ancients tended to think of east-west opposites rather than our north-south.

vocabulary

coma (1) *foliage*
dīco, -ere *to mention, tell of*
insignis, -e (adj.) *known for, distinguished by*
intonsus (adj.) *with long hair*
mas, maris (m.) *a male, boy*

nātālis, -e (adj.) *of one's birth*
penitus (adj.) *deeply*
suprēmus (adj.) *highest, mightiest*
tollo, -ere *to extol*
totidem (adv.) *as many times*

POEM 3 (III 6)
(Alcaic)

delicta maiorum immeritus lues,
Romane, donec templa refeceris,
    sedesque labentes deorum et
        foeda nigro simulacra fumo.

5   dis te minorem quod geris, imperas:
hinc omne principium, huc refer exitum.
    di multa neglecti dederunt
        Hesperiae mala luctuosae.

grieving

    iam bis Monaeses et Pacori manus
10   non auspicatos contudit impetus
    nostros et adiecisse praedam
        torquibus exiguis renidet.

necklaces
meagre ornaments

Kings of Parthia 40-36 BC

    paene occupatam seditionibus
delevit urbem Dacus et Aethiops,
15   hic classe formidatus, ille
        missilibus melior sagittis.

Antony used Dacian boatmen
Cleopatra used Ethiopians in the fleet at Actium

    fecunda culpae saecula nuptias
primum inquinavere et genus et domos:
    hoc fonte derivata clades
20   in patriam populumque fluxit.

polluted

cont.

    This ode can be considered as a state poem as well as one dealing with religion. It supports two points in Augustus' policy of social and moral reform. One was the refurbishing of neglected temples; the other involved measures to strengthen the institution of marriage and so arrest a decline in morals.
    The poem is in five sections:
(1) the gods are angry at your neglect of them (lines 1-8);
(2) this has led to military defeats and near defeats (lines 9-16);
(3) it has also led to loose morals both before and after marriage (lines 17-32);

(4) it was the clean, tough life of the early Romans that made us invincible (lines 33-44);

(5) each generation now seems worse than the one before it (lines 45-48).

We cannot know if Horace believed lines 1-8. He almost certainly did *not* believe in the Olympian gods, but who can say for sure that he did not at times feel that there was a 'divinity that shapes our ends'? This would clash with his Epicurean outlook but Horace never claims to be a consistent philosopher.

We may feel there is some hypocrisy in the censure of morals since Horace had undoubtedly sown a few wild oats in his time. But his affairs were with courtesans and do not prevent him from honestly deploring the fact that Roman matrons should imitate such women.

His praise of the Romans of old is obviously sincere. The freshness of the sturdy Sabine farmer stock is in glorious contrast to the cheap debaucheries in many of the marriages of his day. He ends on a note of rather hackneyed pessimism: things aren't what they were and they'll be worse before they get better.

The poem contains various historical allusions: (lines 9-12) Pacorus and Monaeses, kings of Parthia, won small victories over lieutenants of Antony (40-36 B.C.); (lines 13-16) at Actium Antony used bowmen from Dacia, and Ethiopians served in Cleopatra's fleet; (line 33) the Romans scored naval victories over the Carthaginians at Mylae in 260 B.C. and at the Aegates Islands in 241 B.C.; (line 34) Antiochus, king of Syria, was defeated by L. Scipio in 190 B.C.; (line 35-36) Pyrrhus from Epirus in north-western Greece threatened Italy but was defeated in 275 B.C., Hannibal ravaged Italy from 218 to 203 B.C. but lost the battle of Zama in North Africa in 202 B.C.

notes

1. immeritus, 'innocent'. The blame belongs to the earlier generation which had allowed the neglect.
5. dis, ablative of comparison. 6. hinc . . . huc, 'from this' (obeying the gods) . . . 'to this' (ceasing to obey).
10. non auspicatos . . . impetus, 'ill-omened attacks'; because the gods were angry. 11-12. adiecisse . . . renidet, 'smiles to have added', 'is delighted to have added'. torquibus exiguis, this contemptuous description would suit half-naked savages rather than the Parthians.
13. paene, with *delevit*. seditionibus, the Civil Wars. 15. hic . . . ille, 'the latter' . . . 'the former'.
17-32. This is meant to shock; it does not mean that every Roman husband and wife behaved like this! 18. primum, 'first', *i.e.* the pollution of family life was the start of the rot.

[*for vocabulary see p. 15*]

motus doceri gaudet Ionicos
matura virgo et fingitur artibus
   iam nunc et incestos amores
      de tenero meditatur ungui;

25   mox iuniores quaerit adulteros
inter mariti vina, neque eligit
   cui donet impermissa raptim
      gaudia luminibus remotis,

sed iussa coram non sine conscio
30   surgit marito, seu vocat institor
   seu navis Hispanae magister,
      dedecorum pretiosus emptor.

non his iuventus orta parentibus
infecit aequor sanguine Punico
35   Pyrrhumque et ingentem cecidit
      Antiochum Hannibalemque dirum;

sed rusticorum mascula militum
proles, Sabellis docta ligonibus
   versare glaebas et severae
40   matris ad arbitrium recisos

portare fustes, sol ubi montium
mutaret umbras et iuga demeret
   bobus fatigatis, amicum
      tempus agens abeunte curru.

45   damnosa quid non imminuit dies?
aetas parentum, peior avis, tulit
   nos nequiores, mox daturos
      progeniem vitiosiorem.

[handwritten margin notes:]
260 BC Mylae
241 BC Agates Islands
275 BC Pyrrhus
190 BC Antiochus
218-203 } Hannibal
202

notes continued

21. motus Ionicos, 'eastern Greek dance movements', with lewdness implied; dancing was not considered suitable for free-born Roman girls. **22. fingitur artibus**, 'she is trained in all the arts' (of attracting men). **23. iam nunc**, 'even now', at her tender age. **24. de tenero . . . ungui**, variously translated, 'from the heart', 'from top to toe', 'from childhood'.

26. inter mariti vina, 'at her husband's drinking parties'. **neque eligit**, '*she does not choose*', *i.e.* her husband acts as procurer.

29-30. coram non sine conscio . . . marito, a mixture of *coram marito* 'in the presence of her husband' and *non sine conscio marito* 'with the full knowledge of her husband'. **30-31 institor . . . magister**, they would both have goods from abroad to offer in payment.

33. non his . . ., very emphatic, 'it was not from parents like *these . . .*'. **35.** *caedo, cecīdi* should be distinguished from *cado, cecĭdi*.

37. rusticorum . . . militum, when a farmer left his plough and took up the sword; before the days of a professional army. **38. Sabellis**, the Sabines are typical of tough peasant stock; Cicero calls them *robur rei publicae*. **40. ad arbitrium** (with genitive), 'at the orders of'.

41. fustes, sticks for threshing grain. **42. mutaret . . . demeret**, subjunctive as still part of the mother's orders. **43. bobus**, dative plural of *bos*. **44. agens**, agrees with *sol*. **abeunte curru**, the Sun-god drives his chariot up, then away down the sky.

45. dies, feminine 'time'. **46. aetas**, here = 'the generation', so *aetas parentum* 'the people who lived in our parents' days'. **47. daturos**, with *nos*, 'about to produce'.

vocabulary

aedes, -is (f.) *temple*
amīcus (adj.) *pleasant*
avus (m.) *grandfather*
culpa (1) *sin*
damnōsus (adj.) *ruinous*
dēdecus, oris (n) *deed of shame*
exitus, -ūs (m.) *end, result*
fēcundus (+ gen.) *rich in*
fluo, -ere, fluxi *to flow*
se gero, -ere *to show oneself*
glaeba (1) *clod of earth*
Hesperia (1) *Italy*
imminuo, -ere *to weaken*
infīcio, -ere, -ēci *to stain*
inquino (1) *to pollute*
institor, -ōris (m.) *pedlar*

lābor, -i *to fall, decay*
ligo, -ōnis (m.) *mattock, hoe*
luo, -ere *to pay for, expiate*
magister, -ri (m.) *captain*
maiōres, -um (pl.) *ancestors*
manus, -ūs (f.) *band of men*
nēquior (adj.) *more worthless, baser*
pretiōsus (adj.) *extravagant*
principium (n.) *beginning*
prōles, -is (f.) *race, breed*
recīdo, -ere, -īdi, -īsum *to cut*
refero, -ferre *to ascribe*
Sabellus (adj.) *Sabine*
torquis, -is (m.) *necklace*
verso (1) *to loosen, turn over*

POEM 4 (I 34)
(Alcaic)

parcus deorum cultor et infrequens
insanientis dum sapientiae
   consultus erro, nunc retrorsum
      vela dare atque iterare cursus

abandoned

5   cogor relictos: namque Diespiter
igni corusco nubila dividens
   plerumque, per purum tonantes
      egit equos volucremque currum,

whereby

    quo bruta tellus et vaga flumina,
10   quo Styx et invisi horrida Taenari
   sedes Atlanteusque finis
      concutitur. valet ima summis

mutare et insignem attenuat deus,
obscura promens; hinc apicem rapax
15   Fortuna cum stridore acuto
      sustulit, hic posuisse gaudet.

This ode marks one of the many swings in Horace's thoughts about religion and philosophy. He has heard thunder from a clear sky and this makes him reflect that after all there must be a god up in the sky who controls mortal destinies. This contradicts the basic Epicurean belief that natural causes, not supernatural intervention, can explain all the phenomena of the world of nature.

Horace was probably sincere when he wrote this, but we need not believe that his conversion was a permanent one. Some, indeed, treat the whole poem as humorous.

notes

2. insanientis . . . sapientiae, oxymoron, 'wisdom that is no wisdom'. **3. consultus** (with gen.), 'experienced in', 'steeped in'. **4. vela dare**, 'to sail'. **iterare**, 'to retrace', 'go back over again'.

6. igni, ablative. **7.** note the emphatic position of *plerumque*. **per purum**, 'in a cloudless sky'.

10. Taenari, a deep cave near Cape Taenarum was supposed to be one way down to the Underworld. **11. Atlanteus finis**, 'the boundary formed by Mt Atlas'. The Atlas Mts. and Straits of Gibraltar formed the western boundary of the known world. **12. ima summis**, neuter plurals, 'to change the lowest for the highest'.

14. apicem, *apex* is properly a priest's cap, here a diadem or crown. **15. Fortuna**, the Romans were fond of the goddess Luck, here visualised as a bird. **16. sustulit**, 'has removed'.

vocabulary

attenuo (1) *to lessen, degrade*
brutus (adj.) *massive, solid*
cultor, -oris (c) *worshipper*
cursus (4) *course*
Diespiter *Jupiter*
divido (3) *to split, cleave*
invisus (adj.) *hated, hateful*

parcus (adj.) *moderate*
promo (3) *to bring forward*
retrorsum (adv.) *backwards*
tellus, -uris (f.) *earth*
valeo (2) *to have power (to)*
volucris, -e (adj.) *flying*

POEM 5 (III 2)
(Alcaic)

angustam amice pauperiem pati
robustus acri militia puer
    condiscat et Parthos feroces
        vexet eques metuendus hasta

5   vitamque sub divo et trepidis agat
in rebus. illum ex moenibus hosticis
    matrona bellantis tyranni
        prospiciens et adulta virgo

suspiret, eheu, ne rudis agminum
10   sponsus lacessat regius asperum
    tactu leonem, quem cruenta
        per medias rapit ira caedes.

provoke (l. 10 margin note)

dulce et decorum est pro patria mori:
mors et fugacem persequitur virum,
15   nec parcit imbellis iuventae
        poplitibus timidoque tergo.

transitional negative definition? l. 13 (margin note)

virtus repulsae nescia sordidae
intaminatis fulget honoribus,
    nec sumit aut ponit secures
20   arbitrio popularis aurae.

virtus, recludens immeritis mori
caelum, negata temptat iter via,
    coetusque vulgares et udam
        spernit humum fugiente pinna.

(*cont.*

This poem is in the form of a Stoic hymn to *virtus* as both physical courage and moral perfection. The Stoic philosopher, the *sapiens,* is possessed of *virtus* in both meanings and for him it is the only good. All other things (pain, death, pleasure, popularity, etc.) are indifferent and can be chosen or avoided

only if this does not interfere with virtue. The Stoic accepted a
duty to the State and moral obligations.

Lines 1-16 speak of courage in battle and were in harmony
with Augustus' efforts to revive old Roman virtues. Lines 17-32
are less obvious. They refer to *virtus* as the prime civic virtue
which can raise a man even as high as Olympus, just as its
opposite can bring inevitable punishment.

notes

1. amice, 'in a friendly way', *i.e.* accepting poverty as one would a friend. **2.
robustus**, with ablative 'hardened by'. **4. eques**, 'as a cavalryman'.
5. sub divo, 'in the open'. **6.** the order is *matrona . . . et virgo . . . prospiciens
. . . illum . . . suspiret . . . .* **7. matrona**, the wife of the *tyrannus* and mother of
the betrothed *virgo*.
10. sponsus regius, 'her royal fiancé'. **asperum tactu**, 'rough to touch',
'hard to handle'. **11. leonem**, the *robustus puer* of line 2. **12. rapit**, his anger
'carries him along'.
14. et, 'also' with *fugacem virum*. **16. poplitibus**, *poples* is the back of the knee
joint; the reference is to wounds received in flight.
17. virtus, 'manliness', 'true worth'; here in civilian life. **nescia**, 'ignorant
of'; because to a Stoic such things are indifferent. **18. honoribus**, 'positions
of honour', 'magistracies'. **19. ponit**, for **deponit**, 'lays down'. **secures**,
'axes' symbols of authority. **20. popularis aurae**, since the favour of the mob
is as unpredictable as wind direction.
21. immeritis mori, 'for those who do not deserve to die'. **22. negata . . .
via**, 'on a road denied (to ordinary men)'. **temptat iter**, 'attempts a route',
i.e. 'dares to tread'. **23. udam**, the contrast is between the soggy earth and
the clear regions into which *virtus* can soar.

(*for vocabulary see p.21*)

25   est et fideli tuta silentio
        merces: vetabo, qui Cereris sacrum
        vulgarit arcanae, sub isdem
           sit trabibus fragilemque mecum

        solvat phaselon. saepe Diespiter
30   neglectus incesto addidit integrum;
        raro antecedentem scelestum
           deseruit pede Poena claudo.

Augustus as *pontifex maximus,* from a full length statue of the late first century
B.C., Museo Nazionale delle Terme, Rome.

(*notes continued*)

25-32. there is a sure reward for him who does not speak of religious mysteries and a slow but sure punishment for him who reveals them – avoid such a man! **25. et** as in line 14. **26. vetabo,** supply (*eum*) *qui* . . . (*ut*) *sit* . . . . **27. arcanae,** translate with *sacrum*.

29. phaselon, Greek accusative for Latin *phaselum*. **30. incesto** . . . **integrum,** masculine; Jupiter can make mistakes so watch your step! **31. raro,** 'rarely' contrasted with *saepe,* line 29. **32. deseruit,** 'has failed to catch', *i.e.* the mills of God grind slowly but . . . surely.

vocabulary

adultus (adj.) *grown up*

angustus (adj.) *constricting*

arbitrium (2) *decision*

arcānus (adj.) *secret*

bello (1) *to be at war*

claudus (adj.) *lame*

coetus (4) *assembly, crowd*

condisco (3) *to learn well*

cruentus (adj.) *bloodthirsty*

decōrus (adj.) *comely, proper*

humus (f.) *earth*

imbellis (adj.) *unwarlike, feeble*

intāminātus (adj.) *unspotted*

integer (adj.) *pure, innocent*

mercēs, -ēdis (f.) *reward*

phasēlus (2) *boat* (see on 29 above)

reclūdo (3) *to open up*

repulsa (1) *election defeat*

rudis (adj.) (+ gen.) *unskilled in*

sacrum (2) *holy rite*

suspīro (1) *to sigh*

trabes (pl.) *roof*

trepidus (adj.) *dangerous*

vulgo (1) *to reveal, make public*

POEM 6 (II 3)
(Alcaic)

aequam memento rebus in arduis
servare mentem, non secus in bonis
    ab insolenti temperatam
        laetitia, moriture Delli,

5   seu maestus omni tempore vixeris,
seu te in remoto gramine per dies
    festos reclinatum bearis
        interiore nota Falerni.

ecumenical
evocative

    quo pinus ingens albaque populus
10   umbram hospitalem consociare amant
    ramis? quid obliquo laborat   *strives to scurry*
        lympha fugax trepidare rivo?

instrumental ablative

red
&
black
&
yellow   *fortune*

    huc vina et unguenta et nimium breves   *prepare*
    flores amoenae ferre iube rosae,   *a Symposium*
15   dum res et aetas et sororum
        fila trium patiuntur atra.

(cont.

This poem contains a lot of the essential Horace. The main message is Epicurean. Let the things of the world bother you as little as possible. Enjoy life to the full since all pleasure, all sensation ceases at death which is inevitable.

The first stanza has an echo of the poet's favourite Golden Mean theme. Don't be *too* cast down in adversity or *too* elated in prosperity.

Lines 9-12 reveal Horace's deep appreciation of the countryside, see Section IV below.

Petronius speaks of Horace's *curiosa felicitas*. If he had merely called him *curiosus* (diligent, painstaking), he would be dismissing him as uninspired. But he adds *felicitas* (success) to show that the hours spent on rhythm, word order, choice of words, etc. do not show in the finished product. There is no smell of midnight oil. The poem reads as though it had flowed forth spontaneously and could be expressed in no other way.

A number of points should be particularly noted: the first word *aequam*, setting the mood equanimity; the brutally emphatic *cedes . . . cedes* (lines 17 and 19) and *omnes . . . omnium* (line 25); the elisions in line 10 which draw the trees together; the marvellously evocative *cogimur* (line 25) – 'we are rounded up (like sheep)' (cf. *coerces* in Poem 1 line 18 and *compulerit* in Poem 15 line 18); the beautiful *obliquo laborat lympha fugax trepidare rivo* of a fast-running stream that darts from side to side to pass obstacles.

notes

2. non secus, 'and in the same way'. **3. temperatam**, *temperare ab* = 'to restrain oneself from (something)'. **4. moriture**, to be taken closely with *seu . . . seu*.

7. bearis, future perfect; *te beare* = 'to enjoy yourself'. **8. interiore**, from the back of the store-cupboard, hence 'older'. **Falerni**, 'Falernian', a choice wine from Campania.

9-11. quo . . . quid, 'to what purpose' . . . 'why', implying 'if we don't make use of them'. **11. laborat . . . trepidare**, 'strives to bustle along'.

13. huc, into the shade, by the stream. **15. dum . . .** , we are to enjoy ourselves while three things permit, *res* 'fortune', *aetas* 'our age' and *filum* 'the life-span' alloted by the three sister-Fates (Clotho, Lachesis and Atropos) who spin the thread of life.

(*for vocabulary see p. 25*)

24

cedes coemptis saltibus et domo
villaque, flavus quam Tiberis lavit,
cedes, et exstructis in altum
20   divitiis potietur heres.

divesne prisco natus an Inacho,
nil interest, an pauper et infima
de gente sub divo moreris,
victima nil miserantis Orci:

"eodem"
euphemism for
"to the underworld"

25   omnes eodem cogimur, omnium
versatur urna serius ocius   sooner or later
sors exitura et nos in aeternum
exsilium impositura cumbae.

The lot about to come out
is turned in the urn and
about to put us aboard to raft
to eternal exile

Epicurus, the Greek philosopher (342-270 B.C.), Roman copy from a Greek
portrait statue of the late second century B.C., Metropolitan Museum of Art,
New York (no. 11.90).

notes continued

19. in altum, 'sky-high'.

21-23. the construction is *nil interest divesne (sis)* . . . *an* . . . *moreris,* 'it doesn't matter whether you are . . . or live . . . . **Inacho,** an old king of Argos. **22. infima de gente,** 'from the lowest social class'. **23. sub divo,** 'in the open air'. **24. victima,** supply *eris-* 'you will end up as a victim of . . .'.

26-29. the ancients cast lots by putting pebbles into an urn and rotating it quickly until one jumped out. **26. serius ocius,** 'sooner or later'. **28. cumbae,** dative; Charon's boat which carried the dead over the River Styx.

vocabulary

aequus (adj.) *undisturbed*
brevis (adj.) *shortlived*
cēdo (3) (+ abl.) *depart from*
coemo (3) *to buy up*
consocio (1) *to join, unite*
eōdem (adv.) *to the same place*
filum (2) *thread*
impōno (3) *to put aboard*
insolens, -entis (adj.) *excessive*
nota (1) *brand*

oblīquus (adj.) zig-zag
Orcus (2) *Hades, death*
pōpulus (f.) *poplar tree*
potior (4) (+ abl.) *to get possession of*
rivus (2) *stream, course*
saltus (4) *pasture-land*
sors, sortis (f.) *lot*
verso (1) *to turn, spin, rotate*

POEM 7 (II 10)
(Sapphic)

rectius vives, Licini, neque altum
semper urgendo neque, dum procellas
cautus horrescis, nimium premendo
    litus iniquum.

5   auream quisquis mediocritatem
diligit tutus, caret obsoleti
sordibus tecti, caret invidenda
    sobrius aula.

saepius ventis agitatur ingens
10   pinus et celsae graviore casu
decidunt turres feriuntque summos
    fulgura montes.

sperat infestis, metuit secundis
alteram sortem bene praeparatum
15   pectus. informes hiemes reducit
    Iuppiter, idem

summovet. non, si male nunc, et olim
sic erit: quondam cithara tacentem
suscitat Musam neque semper arcum
20   tendit Apollo.

rebus angustis animosus atque
fortis appare; sapienter idem
contrahes vento nimium secundo
    turgida vela.

This cry for moderation, the Golden Mean, expresses one of the few beliefs that Horace held seriously. He may veer from one philosophy to another, he may believe in God one moment and show no interest the next, but he often repeats the warning not to carry anything too far. This ode is the major statement of the creed.

It warns against excessive recklessness (lines 1-4), excessive ostentation (lines 6-8), too much ambition (lines 9-12), excessive optimism or pessimism (lines 13-15). Then follow the two extremes of weather (lines 15-17), of luck (lines 17-18) and of Apollo's temperament (lines 18-20).

The poem is addressed to Licinius Murena. He was noted for his immoderate freedom of speech, so perhaps Horace is giving him a hint. Murena was later put to death for plotting against Augustus. Perhaps lines 9-12 are telling him to curb his republican sentiments and not aim too high!

notes

1. rectius, *rectus* means 'living according to the rule (*regula*) of a philosophical school'; so *rectius* – 'in a more truly philosophical manner'.
6. tutus, translate 'safely'. **7. invidenda,** 'envy-provoking'. **8. sobrius,** another philosophical term – 'moderate', 'temperate', used of one who observes the Golden Mean.
13. infestis . . . secundis, neuter ablative plurals, supply *in* – 'when things are dangerous' . . . 'when things are favourable'. **14. alteram sortem,** 'the opposite turn of fortune'. **bene praeparatum pectus,** *i.e.* the heart well-prepared by the teachings of philosophy to accept the ups and downs of life. **16. idem,** 'the same man', 'he also'.
17. si male (est), literally 'if it is badly' = 'if things are going badly'. **18-20.** Apollo can either appear as the genial lover of music or as the angry bowman bringing pestilence and death.
21. rebus angustis, 'when things are critical'. **22. appare,** imperative of *appareo*, 'to show oneself'. **sapienter,** the *sapiens* is the perfect philosopher. **idem,** 'you also', see line 16 above.

vocabulary

altum (n.) *the deep, open sea*
aula (1) *palace*
careo (2) (+ abl.) *to avoid*
contraho (3) *to furl*
dīligo (3) *to love*
informis (adj.) *horrid*
inīquus (adj.) *dangerous*
mediōcritas, -ātis (f.) *mean, moderation*
obsolētus (adj.) *broken down*
premo (3) *to keep close to*
quondam (adv.) *sometimes*
sordes, -ium (f.pl.) *squalor*
tendo (3) *to stretch, bend*
urgeo (2) *to press on into, make for*

28

POEM 8 (I 22)
(Sapphic)

integer vitae scelerisque purus
non eget Mauris iaculis neque arcu
nec venenatis gravida sagittis,
    Fusce, pharetra,

5   sive per Syrtes iter aestuosas,
sive facturus per inhospitalem
Caucasum vel quae loca fabulosus
    lambit Hydaspes.

namque me silva lupus in Sabina,
10   dum meam canto Lalagen et ultra
terminum curis vagor expeditis,
    fugit inermem.

quale portentum neque militaris
Daunias latis alit aesculetis,
15   nec Iubae tellus generat, leonum
    arida nutrix.

pone me, pigris ubi nulla campis
arbor aestivā recreatur aurā,
quod latus mundi nebulae malusque
20   Iuppiter urget;

pone sub curru nimium propinqui
solis in terra domibus negata:
dulce ridentem Lalagen amabo,
    dulce loquentem.

brood

revives

The first two lines of this ode found their way into Shakespeare's *Titus Andronicus*. It was often sung as a hymn and, as Wilkinson tells us (*Horace and his Lyric Poetry*), it was intoned over the dead in Swedish graveyards! The usual interpretation is as follows: 'the righteous man needs no weapons to protect him. I know this because, though I was unarmed, a huge wolf fled from me. Wherever I am, I need have no fear. I can sing of the sweet voice and smile of my lady love'.

But surely this poem is not meant to be taken seriously. The deliberate descent from the lofty ethics at the beginning to dalliance with his favourite courtesan should rather be taken as beautifully contrived bathos. The description of the wolf in the fourth stanza is a mock-heroic magnifying of the danger. And, most convincing of all, can we really imagine Horace saying, like Sir Galahad, 'My strength is as the strength of ten because my heart is pure'? We should perhaps envisage Fuscus, a close friend of Horace, looking serious at the first two stanzas and then, as he read on, smiling to hear Horace say, 'Nothing can touch *me*. I'm too good!'.

Some say that Horace claims divine protection here because he is a poet. This is true elsewhere (cf. *di me tuentur,* I 17) and Horace is well aware of the majesty of his calling. But this ode claims immunity because of the writer's virtue and makes only the vaguest of reference to him as a poet.

A noteworthy feature of this poem is the display of geographical knowledge, of which the Roman poets were fond. Six places are named: *Mauris* (line 2), Moorish; *Syrtes* (line 5), quicksands off the North African coast; *Caucasus* (line 7), mountains in Southern Russia; *Hydaspes* (line 8), a river in Pakistan; *Daunias* (line 14), part of Apulia in Southern Italy; *Iubae tellus* (line 15), the land of (King) Juba, *i.e.* Numidia in North Africa.

notes

1. Horace is fond of adjectives with genitive – 'innocent in life and clear of crime'; *cf. consultus* (Poem 4, line 3).

10. Lalagen, her name (*Lalage*) is Greek and means 'chatterer'; cf. *dulce loquentem* line 24. **11. terminum,** the boundary of his Sabine farm. **12. fugit,** here transitive, 'fled from'. **inermem,** in emphatic position, agrees with *me* (line 9).

13. militaris, 'producing good soldiers'. **15. leonum . . . nutrix,** the Roman amphitheatre was supplied with lions from North Africa.

19-20. malus Iuppiter, 'lowering sky', 'bad weather'.

22. domibus negata, 'denied to homes', *i.e.* in the torrid zone where one would not build houses. **23. dulce,** translated as adverb 'sweetly'.

vocabulary

aesculētum (n.) *oak forest*
aestuōsus (adj.) *stormy*
egeo (2) (+ abl.) *to need*
expedio (4) *to release*
fābulōsus (adj.) *famed in story*
genero (1) *to produce*
gravidus (adj.) (+ abl.) *filled with*

lambo (3) *to wash, flow through*
latus, -eris (n.) *side, quarter*
nutrix (f.) *nurse*
piger (adj.) *lifeless*
portentum (n.) *monster*
ultra (+ acc.) *beyond*
urgeo (2) *to oppress*

latus, -a, -um
broad, wide,
expansive

one of the greatest

POEM 9 (I 9)
(Alcaic)

made higher by deep snow

26 mi
42 km.

vides ut altā stet nive candidum
Soracte, nec iam sustineant onus
   silvae laborantes geluque *straining*
     flumina constiterint acuto?

nipping cold & sharp ice

sharp/piercing

dispel

5 dissolve frigus ligna super foco
  large reponens atque benignius
   deprome quadrimum Sabina,
     o Thaliarche, merum diota.

a Greek note

  permitte divis cetera, qui simul
10 stravere ventos aequore fervido
   deproeliantes, nec cupressi
     nec veteres agitantur orni.

  quid sit futurum cras, fuge quaerere, et
  quem fors dierum cumque dabit, lucro
"credit to your account"
15   appone, nec dulces amores
young men dancing in a ring
     sperne puer neque tu choreas,

  donec virenti canities abest
  morosa. nunc et campus et areae
Campus Martius (?)
   lenesque sub noctem susurri
20   composita repetantur hora,

austere diction
intricate word order
 but sentimental subject

  nunc et latentis proditor intimo *juxtaposition*
  gratus puellae risus ab angulo
   pignusque dereptum lacertis
     aut digito male pertinaci.

mischievously resisting

The main message here is to enjoy youth while it lasts. Forget about the frost outside, pile up the fire and bring out the best wine. Forget about tomorrow, remember that you're only young once and take your fill of love and the other pleasures of youth.

The beginning of the ode is an imitation of Alcaeus, but Horace develops it in his own style, ending, as he often does, on a light note. Here it is a girl giggling from a dark corner.

In this short poem Horace manages to combine nature, philosophy and love and swings from the serious to the light and humorous.

notes

isolated Ridge, separated from Sabine mountains by Tiber

2. Soracte, a mountain north of Rome and a prominent landmark. **3. laborantes,** the trees toil under their weight of snow. **4. constiterint,** 'cease flowing'.
6. benignius, 'more generously'. **8. Thaliarche,** probably an invented name signifying one in the bloom of youth.
9. simul, for *simul ac,* 'as soon as'. **11. deproeliantes,** 'struggling with one another'.
13. fuge quaerere, imperative + infinitive – 'avoid asking'. **14. quem . . . dierum cumque,** for *quemcumque dierum* – either 'whatever sort of day' or 'whatever number of days'. **lucro appone,** 'put down as a gain'. **16. puer,** 'while you are young'.
17. virenti, supply *tibi* – 'from you in the freshness of youth'.
18-20. The subjects of *repetantur* are *campus, areae, susurri, risus* (line 22) and *pignus* (line 23). **20. composita . . . hora,** 'at the hour agreed'.
21. proditor, with *latentis puellae* and in apposition to *risus.* **24. male pertinaci,** 'badly resisting', *i.e.* resisting feebly, putting up a token resistance.

vocabulary

ārea (1) *a playground*
campus (2) *exercise-ground*
cānitiēs (f.) grey hair, old age
chorēa (1) *a dance*
dēprōmo (3) *to fetch out*
dēripio, -ere, -ui, dereptum *to snatch from*
diōta (1) *a two-handled jar*
fervidus (adj.) *boiling*
fors (f.) *chance, luck*

gelu (4.n.) *frost*
intimus (adj.) *inmost*
largē (adv.) *plentifully*
mōrōsus (adj.) *peevish*
ornus (f.) *mountain-ash*
pignus (n.) *a love-token*
quadrīmus (adj.) *four years old*
sterno, ere, strāvi *to make smooth*
susurrus (2) *a whisper*

POEM 10 (I 11)
(Asclepiad System 5)

tu ne quaesieris – scire nefas – quem mihi,
    quem tibi
finem di dederint, Leuconoe, nec
    Babylonios
temptaris numeros. ut melius, quidquid
    erit, pati,
seu plures hiemes seu tribuit Iuppiter
    ultimam,
5   quae nunc oppositis debilitat pumicibus
    mare
Tyrrhenum. sapias, vina liques et spatio
    brevi
spem longam reseces. dum loquimur,
    fugerit invida
aetas: carpe diem, quam minimum
    credula postero.

The message in this poem is similar to that in Poem 9. Leuconoe is told not to consult astrologers to find the future. Enjoy today as though it were your last day on earth. Even as we speak our time is running out. *Carpe diem* (line 8) has been a motto for hedonists ever since it was written.

Horace is deadly serious in this poem. He loved life and was desperately anxious to use every minute of it before death put an end to all.

notes

1-3. ne quaesieris . . . nec . . . temptaris, for *quaesiveris, temptaveris; ne* with perfect subjunctive is a polite form of prohibition. **2. Babylonios . . . numeros,** the calculations made by Babylonian astrologers in casting a horoscope. **3. ut melius,** *ut* is here exclamatory: 'how much better it is to . . . '. **5.** the winter 'weakens' the sea by making it spend its strength dashing on the rocks. **6. sapias . . . liques . . . reseces,** 2nd person singular present subjunctives used as commands. **spatio brevi,** ablative absolute. **7. fugerit,** future perfect. **8. carpe diem,** 'pluck the day' *i.e.* enjoy it like a flower before it withers.

vocabulary

crēdulus (adj. + dat.) *trusting in*
invidus (adj.) *envious, grudging*
liquo (1) *to strain*
pŭmices (pl.) *rocks*

reseco (1) *to prune, cut back*
spatium (2) *life-span*
tempto (1) *to make trial of*

POEM 11 (IV 7)
(Hexameter and Archilochius Minor)

diffugere nives, redeunt iam gramina campis
    arboribusque comae,

mutat terra vices et decrescentia ripas
    flumina praetereunt,

5   Gratia cum Nymphis geminisque sororibus audet
    ducere nuda choros.

immortalia ne speres, monet annus et almum
    quae rapit hora diem.

frigora mitescunt Zephyris, ver proterit aestas,
10   interitura, simul

pomifer autumnus fruges effuderit, et mox
    bruma recurrit iners.

damna tamen celeres reparant caelestia lunae:
    nos, ubi decidimus,

15   quo pater Aeneas, quo Tullus dives et Ancus,
    pulvis et umbra sumus.

quis scit an adiciant hodiernae crastina summae
    tempora di superi?

cuncta manus avidas fugient heredis, amico
20   quae dederis animo.

cum semel occideris et de te splendida Minos
    fecerit arbitria,

non, Torquate, genus, non te facundia, non te
    restituet pietas:

25   infernis neque enim tenebris Diana pudicum
    liberat Hippolytum,

nec Lethaea valet Theseus abrumpere caro
    vincula Pirithoo.

There are four themes in this poem. All of them are echoed elsewhere; for Horace is so serious on the subject of the brevity of life that he repeats these ideas in different forms:

(1) the year dies and is reborn, moons wane and wax, but for us there is no such resurrection (cf. Odes I 4 and see Catullus 5);

(2) we cannot know which day will be our last (cf. Poem 9 lines 13-15 and Poem 10 line 4);

(3) nothing can rescue us from Hades (cf. Poem 6 lines 22-24, Poem 12 lines 2-7 and Poem 15 lines 13-15);

(4) use the good things of life or some fortune-hunting heir will use them for you (cf. Poem 6 lines 19-20 and Poem 12 lines 25-28).

This poem has been variously described as 'an unimportant spring-song' and 'the most perfect poem in the Latin language'. It certainly cannot be both. The reader must decide which verdict to accept.

The mythological references in the poem are as follows: *Gratia* (line 5), the three Graces (*Gratia . . . cum geminis sororibus*), goddesses of beauty, also associated with the arts; *Nymphis* (line 5), nymphs, minor goddesses of nature inhabiting ocean, streams, mountains, forests; *Zephyris* (line 9), *Zephyrus,* the balmy west wind; *Aeneas* (line 15), a Trojan nobleman, hero of Virgil's *Aeneid* and father of Iulus, founder of the Julian family; *Tullus et Ancus* (line 15), ancient kings of Rome; *Minos* (line 21), son of Jupiter and king of Crete, who after death became a judge in the Underworld; *Diana . . . Hippolytum* (lines 25-26), Hippolytus, dedicated to celibacy and to the virgin goddess Diana, who failed to save him when Venus caused his death for spurning the advances of his step-mother Phaedra; *Lethaea* (line 27), *Lethe,* was one of the rivers of Hades – so the adjective means 'of death'; *Theseus . . . Pirithoo* (lines 27-28), Theseus and Pirithous, close friends, the latter being trapped in Hades when they tried to carry off Persephone, queen of the Underworld.

notes

3. mutat . . . vices, 'renews her changes', *i.e.* one season succeeds another; here winter gives way to spring. 8. hora, 'the passage of time'. 10. simul, for *simul ac*, 'as soon as'. 12. iners, 'stiff', 'frozen': nature is dead as man will be. 13. damna . . . caelestia, 'heavenly losses' – the waning of the moon. celeres, translate as an adverb. 15. quo, supply a verb, 'to where . . . have gone'. 16. pulvis et umbra, dust in the urn, a ghost in Hades. 17. hodiernae . . . summae, dative, 'to today's total'. 19-20. amico quae dederis animo, the nearest we can get is 'which you have given to your own dear self'. 21. occideris, the verb means 'to set', 'to sink' of the heavenly bodies and refers back to lines 13-14. splendida . . . arbitria, 'his noble judgement', 'his royal decision'. 25. neque enim . . . nec, 'for neither did Diana . . . nor Theseus . . . '. 25-27. pudicum . . . caro, each emphasising the main quality of Hippolytus and Pirithous.

vocabulary

almus (adj.) *cheerful, genial*	intereo *to perish*
brūma (1) *winter*	pōmifer (adj.) *fruit-bearing*
coma (1) *foliage*	praetereo (trans.) *to run past*
dēcido (3) *to sink down*	prōtero (3) *to tread down*
diffugio, -ere, -fūgi *to disperse*	spēro (1) *to hope for*
hēres, -ēdis *heir*	

POEM 12 (II 14)
(Alcaic)

eheu fugaces, Postume, Postume,
labuntur anni, nec pietas moram
    rugis et instanti senectae
      adferet indomitaeque morti;

5   non, si trecenis, quotquot eunt dies,
    amice, places inlacrimabilem
      Plutona tauris, qui ter amplum
        Geryonen Tityonque tristi

    compescit unda, scilicet omnibus, *dat q agent*
10   [quicumque terrae munere vescimur,]
      enaviganda, sive reges
        sive inopes erimus coloni.

    frustra cruento Marte carebimus
    fractisque rauci fluctibus Hadriae,
15   frustra per autumnos nocentem
        corporibus metuemus Austrum.

    visendus ater flumine languido
    Cocytos errans et Danai genus
      infame damnatusque longi
20   Sisyphus Aeolides laboris.

                       (cont.

    This is one of the best-known of the Odes and also – and this does not always follow – one of the finest. Even in this uncultured age many people may murmur *eheu fugaces* as they remember some glorious or indiscreet moment from their youth.

    We find here many examples of Horace's effective choice and use of words: the pathetic repetitions *Postume, Postume* and later *frustra . . . frustra*; the happy choice of adjectives *fugaces anni, instanti senectae, inlacrimabilem Plutona, placens uxor, brevem dominum, mero superbo*; the forceful gerundives placed first in the fifth and sixth stanzas. The ideas, as often, are not original but the verbal felicity and a sad seriousness with which most readers can identify make this a memorable poem.

Some may find the mythological references tedious. But it must be remembered that educated Romans were steeped in Greek mythology and appreciated the use of these stories in their literature. There are six references to the Underworld and its inhabitants: *Plutona* (line 7), Greek accusative of *Pluto*, king of the Underworld; *Geryonen* (line 8), Greek accusative of *Geryon*, a triple-bodied monster slain by Heracles; *Tityon* (line 8), Greek accusative of *Tityos*, a huge giant killed for offering violence to Leto and Artemis; *Cocytos* (line 18), the river of lamentation in the Underworld; *Danai genus* (line 18), 49 of the 50 daughters of Danaus, on their father's orders, killed their husbands on the wedding night; *Sisyphus* (line 20), son of Aeolus *(Aeolides)* condemned for ever to push a huge rock up a hill in Hades.

notes

5. quotquot eunt dies, 'as many as the days pass', *i.e.* 'every day'. **7. ter amplum**, 'three-times huge', *i.e.* with three huge bodies.
9. omnibus, dative of agent after *enaviganda* which agrees with *unda*. **10. munere terrae**, 'the gift of the earth', *i.e.* food-crops.
14. fractis . . . fluctibus, 'broken waves', 'breakers'. **Hadriae**, the Adriatic is notoriously rough. **16. Austrum**, the autumn south wind brought sickness *(nocentem corporibus)*.
18. errans, 'flowing slowly', with *flumine languido*. **19. damnatus**, with genitive, 'condemned to'. **Cocytos**, Greek nominative.

(for vocabulary see p.39)

linquenda tellus et domus et placens
uxor, neque harum, quas colis, arborum
te praeter invisas cupressos
ulla brevem dominum sequetur.

25   absumet heres Caecuba dignior
servata centum clavibus et mero
tinguet pavimentum superbo,
pontificum potiore cenis.

Horace, from a contorniate portrait of the fourth century A.D., bearing the inscription ORATIVS; British Museum, London.

notes continued

22. the order is *neque ulla harum . . . arborum te . . . sequetur.* **23. invisas,** because associated with Pluto and so with death.

25. dignior, 'worthier', because he uses the good things and doesn't hoard them. **26. centum clavibus,** humorous exaggeration. **28. pontificum potiore cenis,** 'better than (the wine drunk at) the banquets of priests.

vocabulary

brevis (adj.) *short-lived*
Caecuba (n.pl.) Caecuban wine
careo (2 + abl.) *to avoid*
colōnus (2) *a farmer*
compesco (3) *to keep in, confine*
indomitus (adj.) *unconquerable*
inlacrimābilis (adj.) *impervious to tears*
instans (adj.) *imminent*

lābor (3) *to glide by*
languidus (adj.) *sluggish*
plāco (1) *to placate*
scīlicet *of course, certainly*
tinguo (3) *to stain*
trecēni (adj.) *300-each*
tristis (adj.) *gloomy*
rūgae (1) *wrinkles*
vescor (3 + abl.) *to feed on*

POEM 13 (III 30)
(Asclepiad System 1)

exegi monumentum aere perennius
regalique situ pyramidum altius,
quod non imber edax, non Aquilo impotens
possit diruere aut innumerabilis
5   annorum series et fuga temporum.
non omnis moriar, multaque pars mei
vitabit Libitinam: usque ego postera
crescam laude recens, dum Capitolium
scandet cum tacita virgine pontifex.
10 dicar, qua violens obstrepit Aufidus
et qua pauper aquae Daunus agrestium
regnavit populorum, ex humili potens
princeps Aeolium carmen ad Italos
deduxisse modos. sume superbiam
15 quaesitam meritis et mihi Delphica
lauro cinge volens, Melpomene, comam.

— — | — ∪∪ — | — ∪∪ — | ∪ —

This ode sheds some light upon the Epicurean gloom on the subject of death. Death is inevitable? Yes. There is no return from the Underworld? None. But something *does* survive – the fame a man has won in his lifetime lives on.

Horace is well aware of his eminence as a poet and is sure that this will keep his name alive. In fact he underestimates his fame and its duration. The pontifex has long since ceased to climb the Capitol with the silent Vestal but Horace is still very much with us.

Horace does not here claim to have invented the lyric metres he uses but to have enriched Latin poetry by their introduction. Catullus did try a couple of poems in Sapphic metre but this does not really invalidate Horace's claim.

notes

4-5. innumerabilis . . . temporum, a sonorous phrase, 'the countless succession of the years and the flight of time'. **7. Libitinam**, the Roman goddess of the dead. **usque**, with both *crescam* and *recens*- 'ever I shall grow' and 'ever fresh'. **9. tacita virgine**, a Vestal Virgin; silence was obligatory at religious ceremonies. **10. dicar qua**, 'I shall be spoken of (as one who) where . . .', *i.e.* people will say how one who came from Apulia . . . (the Aufidus was an Apulian river and Daunus an ancient king of Apulia – cf. Poem 8 line 14). **11. pauper aquae**, 'short of water'. **12. populorum**, genitive after *regnavit* – a Greek construction. **13. Aeolium carmen**, the Alcaics, Sapphics etc. of the Odes. **14. deduxisse**, 'to have launched' Greek verse into Latin poetry. **sume superbiam**, 'assume a proud air'; Horace identifies himself with the Muse who inspired his poetry. **15. quaesitam**, 'acquired', 'won'. **Delphica lauro**, the laurel was sacred to Apollo god of poets whose great temple was at Delphi. **16. volens**, 'with a will', 'without hesitation'. **Melpomene**, strictly the Muse of tragedy but simply invoked here as one of the nine Muses.

vocabulary

Aquilo, -ōnis (m.) *the north wind*
edax (adj.) *corroding*
exigo, -ere, -ēgi *to complete*
impotens (adj.) *violent*

merita (n.pl.) *merits, deserts*
posterus (adj.) *of posterity*
princeps (adj.) *first*
situs (4) *structure*

Virgil with the Muses of History and Tragedy, from a Roman mosaic; found at Sousse, Tunisia. (See Poems **14** and **15** below.)

SECTION II

Friends

Horace himself said, 'There is nothing in the world I would compare with a congenial friend', and in this he agrees with his master Epicurus who considered friendship the most durable of earthly acquisitions. Indeed, the cultivation of lasting friendships was characteristic of Epicurus' school.

Sprung, as Horace was, from relatively humble stock, we might expect him to feel inferior in the company of Maecenas and the top Roman social set, but there is no trace of this. Even in writing of Augustus, who became a personal friend, the poet shows respect but never servility. He neither flatters his exalted friends nor allows them to take him for granted. He politely declines to sing of the martial exploits of Agrippa; he excuses himself to Maecenas for being absent from Rome longer than he had promised, but he does so in a manly way. His close friendship with Virgil, who was a shy, withdrawn person, shows that he had a genius for making and keeping friends.

Poems 14 to 18 are full of joy in his friends' company, solicitude for their absence, deep sadness at their death. Horace is seen as one who found more pleasure in men's company than in women's – one reason, perhaps, why he never married; his relations with women are discussed in Section III.

*a propempticon - formal shape dictated by supposition that it
was addressed to someone preparing to sail overseas.
well worn commonplaces about sea.
traditional themes + formulas; formal patterns
vs poet's own immediate feelings + perceptions - which bring the material alive.
how successful is
fusion of the two?*

POEM 14 (I 3)
(Asclepiad System 2)

> sic te diva potens Cypri,
>   sic fratres Helenae, lucida sidera,
> ventorumque regat pater
>   obstrictis aliis praeter Iapyga,
> 5   navis, quae tibi creditum
>   debes Vergilium, finibus Atticis
> reddas incolumem, precor,
>   et serves animae dimidium meae.
>   illi robur et aes triplex
> 10   circa pectus erat, qui fragilem truci
> commisit pelago ratem
>   primus, nec timuit praecipitem Africum
> decertantem Aquilonibus
>   nec tristes Hyadas nec rabiem Noti,
> 15   quo non arbiter Hadriae
>   maior, tollere seu ponere vult freta.

(marginal notes: tired; voc.; metaphor; (ut); word order; juxtaposition; meator 15; than whom; sc. seu; west wind blowing from Italy across adriatic; Iapyx (Greek accusative); Southwest Wind; South Wind)

(cont.

This poem is included in this section on the basis of the first 8 lines.
Horace owed to Virgil and L. Varius the introduction to Maecenas
which changed his whole life. Because of this, and despite their
different temperaments, Horace and Virgil became firm
friends – so much so that Horace describes Virgil here as 'half of
my soul'. Virgil is crossing the Adriatic on his way to Athens and
Horace begs the ship to bring him safely back.

The 32 lines which follow show how Horace develops a theme
with material apparently only losely related to what has gone
before. With typical emotional moderation he does not want to 'go
on' about his affection for Virgil and so he diverges into
mythology. He does not abandon the main purpose of his
poem – that Virgil is aboard ship and may be in danger – for he
speaks of the rash courage of the first mariners who defied the
dangers of the deep. Then, with a reference to Daedalus, 'the first
airman', he asks how we can expect Jupiter to withold disasters
when Man has the temerity to exceed the natural limitations
imposed on him.

Lines 9-40 do not show Horace at his best. The daring of the first
seaman occupies lines 9-24 which contain a rather verbose

*Virgil visited Athens in 19 BC: died on return
is this earlier?*

*8
8 - reflection on man's audacity
8
9 - Prometheus, Daedalus
7 Heracles*

*sea
3 examples of transgression of limits
fire, air, earth*

catalogue of winds and some near repetition between lines 9-14 and 17-20. Lines 25-37 contain an echo of Sophocles' famous chorus in the *Antigone* – 'many are the wonders of the world but there is nothing more wonderful than Man'.

Mythological references are used lavishly:

diva potens Cypri (line 1), Venus, born from the sea off Cyprus; *fratres Helenae* (line 2), Castor and Pollux, twin brothers who protected sailors and were placed in the sky as the constellation *Gemini*; *ventorum . . . pater* (line 3), Aeolus who kept the winds in a cave and made them obey him; *Iapyga* (line 4), Greek accusative of *Iapyx,* a west wind blowing from Italy across the Adriatic; *Hyadas* (line 14), Greek accusative plural of *Hyades,* a constellation which foretold rain and storms; *Iapeti genus* (line 27), Prometheus who stole fire from heaven and gave it to mankind; *Daedalus* (line 34), who, to escape from Crete with his son Icarus, made wings of feathers and wax; *Acheronta* (line 36), Greek accusative of *Acheron,* a river in the Underworld; *Herculeus labor* (line 36), one of the twelve labours of Hercules in which he went to the Underworld and brought up the watchdog Cerberus.

notes

1-8. the construction is *sic te . . . regat, navis . . . (ut) reddas . . . ,* 'may . . . guide you, o ship . . . on condition that you restore . . . '; *precor* is parenthetic. **5. tibi creditum,** 'entrusted to you'. **9-10. illi . . . erat,** 'to that man there was', *i.e.* 'that man had . . . '. **13. decertantem,** 'fighting it out with' – *cf.* Poem 9 line 11. **15. quo non . . . maior,** 'than whom there is no greater . . . '. **Hadriae,** for the roughness of the Adriatic, see Poem 12 line 14.

(for vocabulary see p. 47)

quem Mortis timuit gradum,
    qui siccis oculis monstra natantia,
qui vidit mare turbidum et
20   infames scopulos Acroceraunia?
nequiquam deus abscidit
    prudens Oceano dissociabili
terras, si tamen impiae
    non tangenda rates transiliunt vada.
25   audax omnia perpeti
    gens humana ruit per vetitum nefas:
audax Iapeti genus
    ignem fraude mala gentibus intulit;
post ignem aetheria domo
30   subductum macies et nova febrium
terris incubuit cohors,
    semotique prius tarda necessitas
leti corripuit gradum.
    expertus vacuum Daedalus aera
35   pinnis non homini datis;
    perrupit Acheronta Herculeus labor.
nil mortalibus ardui est;
    caelum ipsum petimus stultitia neque
per nostrum patimur scelus
40   iracunda Iovem ponere fulmina.

notes continued

17. quem . . . gradum, 'what approach of Death did he fear who . . . '. **18. siccis oculis,** 'dry-eyed', with no tears of terror. **20. Acroceraunia,** neuter plural, a rocky promontory dangerous to sailors. **22. prudens,** emphatic – 'in his wisdom'. **25. audax . . . perpeti,** the infinitive completes the meaning – 'bold in enduring'. **28. gentibus,** 'to the races of men'. **30. macies,** 'leanness', 'wasting disease'. **31. terris incubuit,** from *incubo* – 'settled upon the earth'. **32. semoti prius . . . leti,** 'of previously distant death'; early man has always been supposed to have lived to some incredible age. **33. corripuit gradum,** 'has quickened its pace'. **34. expertus (est),** 'made trial of', 'adventured into'. **35. pinnis . . . datis,** *i.e.* it was not Jove's purpose that men should fly. **37. nil . . . ardui,** 'nothing too difficult'; the genitive after such words as *nil, minus, plus, nimis, satis, etc.* is common. **40. iracunda,** transferred epithet: translate with *Iovem*. **ponere,** for *deponere*.

vocabulary

Āfricus (2) *the south-west wind*
Aquilo, -ōnis (m.) *the north wind*
arbiter (2) *master*
dissociābilis (adj.) *separating*
nefas (n.) *impiety, crime*
Notus (2) *the south wind*

obstringo, -ere, -strictum *to tie up*
pōno (3) *to calm* (line 16)
potens (adj. + gen.) *ruling over*
praeceps, -ipitis (adj.) *headlong*
rōbur (n.) *oak-wood*
subdūco (3) *to steal*

Virgil, detail from the relief on the *Ara Pietatis Augustae* of the second quarter of the first century A.D.; Villa Medici, Rome. (For a portrait of Horace set beside Virgil on the same monument, see p.52.)

mourning

POEM 15 (I 24)
(Asclepiad System 3)

quis desiderio sit pudor aut modus
tam cari capitis? praecipe lugubres
cantus, Melpomene, cui liquidam Pater
    vocem cum cithara dedit.

5   ergo Quintilium perpetuus sopor
urget? cui Pudor et Iustitiae soror,
incorrupta Fides, nudaque Veritas
    quando ullum inveniet parem?

multis ille bonis flebilis occidit,
10   nulli flebilior, quam tibi, Vergili.
tu frustra pius, heu, non ita creditum
    poscis Quintilium deos.

quid si Threicio blandius Orpheo
auditam moderere arboribus fidem?
15   non vanae redeat sanguis imagini,
    quam virga semel horrida

non lenis precibus fata recludere
nigro compulerit Mercurius gregi.
durum: sed levius fit patientia
20   quidquid corrigere est nefas.

This poem is a formal elegy or song of mourning, but one which in places bursts the formal bonds. The first stanza is a rather colourless invocation of the Muse. As Page says, it would be better omitted. Then comes grief at the loss of Varus whose qualities can never be replaced. The *ergo . . . urget* is vintage Horace. The third stanza says no one can miss him more than Virgil (to whom the poem is addressed). The suggestion is that Virgil, unlike Horace, believes in the gods but they have let him down. Next comes the irrevocability of death which even the poetic genius of Virgil cannot influence. The last lines are abrupt and very sad. There is no consolation, no expectation of meeting Varus in some Happy

Land. He is dead, he is gone and we must endure his loss with resignation.

We know little of the dead man, Quintilius Varus. He is mentioned in *Ars Poetica* as a stern but honest literary critic who will not tolerate shoddy work. This sincere poetic tribute to him makes us wish we knew him better.

notes

1. pudor, here and in line 6 means 'the feeling that one should not give way to one's emotions'; translate 'restraint', 'moderation'. **3. Melpomene,** the muse of Tragedy and hence here of Elegy.

6. cui, with *parem,* line 8.

9. bonis, masculine. **11. frustra,** with both *pius* and *poscis.* Your piety has brought no reward and you ask for your friend back in vain. **non ita,** not on those terms, *i.e.* not permanently. **12. poscis,** with double accusative.

13-18. read *quid si* (line 13), question mark after *fidem; non* (line 15); full stop after *gregi* (line 18). **13. quid si,** 'what (would happen) if you were to . . .'. **blandius,** 'more winningly than'. **14. auditam . . . arboribus,** 'heard by the trees'; even the trees listened to the music. **15. non redeat** 'would not come back'.

17. non lenis precibus, 'not gentle to prayers', 'impervious to prayers'. **fata recludere,** 'to relax (the decrees of) the fates'. **18. compulerit,** again the idea of Mercury the shepherd rounding up his ghost-sheep (*cf.* Poem 1 line 18). **19-20. levius,** agrees with the *quidquid* clause.

vocabulary

caput, -itis (n.) *person*
compello, -ere, -puli (+ dat.) *to confine in*
crēditus (adj.) *entrusted*
dēsīderium (2) *sense of loss*
ergo (conj.) *and so*
fides (f.) *a lyre* (line 14)

flēbilis (adj. + dat.) *lamented by*
imāgo, -inis (f.) *ghost*
liquidus (adj.) *clear*
moderor (1) *to play* (an instrument)
modus (2) *limit*
patientia (1) *resignation*
praecipio, -ere *to teach*

POEM 16 (III 8)
(Sapphic)

Martiis caelebs quid agam Kalendis
quid velint flores et acerra turis
plena miraris positusque carbo in
    caespite vivo,

5   docte sermones utriusque linguae.
voveram dulces epulas et album
Libero caprum prope funeratus
    arboris ictu.

hic dies anno redeunte festus
10   corticem adstrictum pice dimovebit
amphorae fumum bibere institutae
    consule Tullo.

sume, Maecenas, cyathos amici
sospitis centum et vigiles lucernas
15   perfer in lucem; procul omnis esto
    clamor et ira.

(cont.

lore/learning

ladles

prolong

66 BCE

amici sospitis = your friend safe
= your friend's preservation
noun + adj = abstract idea

Compared with the sadness of Poem 15, this poem is a charming,
light-hearted invitation from Horace to his friend Maecenas which
may be summarised as follows: 'You're probably wondering why a
bachelor like me is throwing a party on Married Women's Day.
Well, on that date I was once nearly "brained" by a falling tree and
I've celebrated it ever since by having friends in and drinking
some of my best wine. Come and drink some with me instead of
sitting at home worrying about political affairs. There's no danger
threatening our country so relax, my friend, and enjoy yourself.'

There is humour throughout this poem (which the light Sapphic metre suits excellently): the colloquial *quid agam* 'what I'm up to'; the mock-pompous *docte sermones utriusque linguae* – even a clever fellow like you can't find the reason for my party; the mock-solemn *funeratus* 'buried with full rites'; *fumum bibere* 'to drink smoke'; the exaggeration in *centum* (line 14). The whole poem is light and shows the excellent relationship between Horace and his eminent friend and patron.

notes

1. Martiis . . . Kalendis, on 1st March married women held a festival in honour of Juno. **quid agam . . . quid velint**, take after *miraris*. **2. quid velint flores**, 'what the flowers mean'. **3-4. carbo . . . vivo**, 'a glowing piece of charcoal on fresh-cut turf', *i.e.* fire on an altar built of turf.
5. docte sermones, retained accusative, 'learnéd in the lore'. **utriusque linguae**, Latin and Greek. **6. album**, emphatic – if he had been killed, a black animal would have been used.
9-12. the cork was sealed with pitch (*adstrictum pice*) and the bottles left to mature in an upper room where smoke from the furnace rose and swirled around them.
11. amphorae, dative with *dimovebit* – 'from the jar'.
13. amici, 'in honour of your friend'. **14. vigiles**, 'sleepless', 'still burning'

(for vocabulary see p. 53)

1. – humorous address in an honorific phrase (docte)
   – humorous macabre: funeratus
2. a series of orders: poet as arbiter bibendi (master of ceremonies)
3. intimate address to Maecenas: worst trouble spots on borders of empire.

Complex – 2 blocks with central connecting stanza
   1-3 preps for a drinking party
   4 party began
   5-7 talking to Maecenas in that setting
creates a setting in which he can urge Maecenas to eat drink & be merry
   but first surveys state of the empire: poetically effective politically serious
then jokes with Maecenas
   then urges hedonistic life of the symposium: "for the moment!"
tone changes; reader must construct a setting from clues
imaginative demand on reader

52

mitte civiles super urbe curas:
occidit Daci Cotisonis agmen,
Medus infestus sibi luctuosis
20   dissidet armis,

are at variance with themselves

servit Hispanae vetus hostis orae
Cantaber sera domitus catena,
iam Scythae laxo meditantur arcu
cedere campis.

lately

25   neglegens, ne qua populus laboret,
parce privatus nimium cavere et
dona praesentis cape laetus horae ac
linque severa.

Horace as a fairly young man, detail from the relief on the *Ara Pietatis Augustae* of the second quarter of the first century A.D.; Villa Medici, Rome. (For Virgil from the same monument, see p.**47**.)

notes continued

17. the date of this ode is uncertain; Maecenas may not have held any office of state at this time but have been concerned for the state as any good citizen would. **18.** the Dacian ruler Cotiso was defeated in 30 B.C. **19-20.** the meaning is that Parthia (*Medus* = Parthian) is in a state of civil war. **sibi,** goes with *infestus* 'dangerous to themselves', with *luctuosis* 'bringing grief to themselves' and with *dissidet* 'are at variance with themselves'. Others take *Medus infestus* = 'our Parthian enemy'.

21-22. vetus hostis . . . sera domitus catena, Romans had been at war in Spain off and on since 217 B.C. **Cantaber,** the Cantabri in North-west Spain were one of the last tribes to be subdued. **Scythae,** nomads from the Russian steppes (*campis*) who sometimes raided Roman territory. **laxo . . . arcu,** 'with loose bow', 'with bow unstrung'.

25. neglegens ne, 'not worrying lest'. **26. privatus,** *i.e.* forgetting state affairs for a while.

vocabulary

acerra (1) *incense-holder*
caelebs (adj.) *unmarried*
ictus (4) *a blow*
institūtus (adj.) *taught*
labōro (1) *to be in trouble*
mitto (3) *to dismiss, banish*
pix, picis (f.) *pitch*

quā (adv.) *in some way*
servio (4) *to be a subject*
sevērus (adj.) *grave, serious*
sospes, -itis (adj.) *safe*
super (+ abl.) *concerning*
tūs, tūris (n.) *incense*

POEM 17 (III 21)
(Alcaic)

o nata mecum consule Manlio,   65 BC.
seu tu querellas sive geris iocos
    seu rixam et insanos amores
        seu facilem, pia testa, somnum,

Complaining quarrels

5   quocumque lectum nomine Massicum
servas, moveri digna bono die,
    descende, Corvino iubente
        promere languidiora vina.

    non ille, quamquam Socraticis madet
10   sermonibus, te negleget horridus:
    narratur et prisci Catonis
        saepe mero caluisse virtus.

    tu lene tormentum ingenio admoves
plerumque duro; tu sapientium
15   curas et arcanum iocoso
        consilium retegis Lyaeo;

    tu spem reducis mentibus anxiis
viresque et addis cornua pauperi,
    post te neque iratos trementi   *dative*
20   regum apices neque militum arma.

    te Liber et, si laeta aderit, Venus
segnesque nodum solvere Gratiae
    vivaeque producent lucernae,
        dum rediens fugat astra Phoebus.

This poem is in the form of jolly hymn to Bacchus and friendship – a good rumbustious poem showing what *Lyaeus* (Bacchus, the 'looser') can do.

    The man addressed, Corvinus, was a soldier, author and patron of literature. He was also a connoisseur of wine. It is typical of

Horace that he does not dwell on Corvinus' good points nor on his friendship for him but makes this poem to a wine-lover into a parody of a prayer – not to a god but to a wine-jar! The prayer form is seen in *quocumque nomine* (in addressing a god one said 'by whatever name you wish to be called') and in the repeated *tu, tu, te*.

notes

1. The vocatives continue to line 6; *o nata . . . pia testa . . . digna* are followed by *descende* (line 7) – 'come down (from the store)'. Manlius was consul in 65 B.C.; this reference gives us the date of Horace's birth.
5. Massicum, a famous wine from Mt. Massicus in Campania. **6. moveri**, this and *descende* and *promere* all refer to taking the jar from the store-cupboard.
9. madet, 'is steeped in', as one might be in wine; *madidus* often means 'drunk'.
11. prisci Catonis, the venerable Cato (died 149 B.C.) was the typical stern old Roman.
13-14. tu . . . duro, rather vague; you gently coax a rather dull, stolid person to come out of himself. **lene tormentum**, 'a gentle torture' wine makes him talk but it's a bit painful for him. **14-16. sapientium curas . . . arcanum consilium**, the first = the problems that worry philosophers, the second = 'a dark secret'; by means of the joker Bacchus the problems become easy and the secret is revealed.
19. post te, 'after drinking you'. **21. te**, with *producent*, 'shall extend you', *i.e.* shall extend the time you are in use. **Liber**, the one who sets free (= Bacchus) as also *Lyaeus* (line 16). **22. segnes nodum solvere**, 'slow to loose the knot'. The three Graces always went together. They are mentioned here because wine increases one's appreciation of beauty. **23. vivae lucernae**, *cf.* Poem 16 lines 14-15.

vocabulary

admoveo (2) *to apply*	**laetus** (adj.) *willingly*
apex, -icis (m.) *a crown*	**languidus** (adj.) *mellow*
caleo (2) *to be aroused*	**lectus** (adj.) *choice*
cornua (n.pl.) *vigour*	**retego** (3) *to lay bare*
gero (3) *to produce*	**testa** (1) *a wine-jar*
horridus (adj.) *uncouth, ascetic*	**tremo** (3) (trans.) *to tremble at*

① Prayer form to wine jar – a surprise (delay)
anaphora – culminates in a generalizing phrase: compare a prayer.
- religious ideas
- blasphemy - descende
- pun madet
- scandalous statement about Cato

③ Praise of the deity – anaphora
preparation for a drinking party: prayer & preparations

POEM 18 (II 7)

(Alcaic)

o saepe mecum tempus in ultimum
deducte Bruto militiae duce,
   quis te redonavit Quiritem
    dis patriis Italoque caelo,

5   Pompei, meorum prime sodalium,
cum quo morantem saepe diem mero
   fregi coronatus nitentes
    malobathro Syrio capillos?

tecum Philippos et celerem fugam
10   sensi relicta non bene parmula,
   cum fracta virtus et minaces
    turpe solum tetigere mento.

sed me per hostes Mercurius celer
denso paventem sustulit aere;
15   te rursus in bellum resorbens
    unda fretis tulit aestuosis.

(cont.

This is a splendid ode full of friendship, humour and genuine feeling. A close friend and fellow-soldier has returned from the wars. They'd always vowed they'd have a big party when they met again and this is it!

Pompeius and Horace had fought on the losing side at the battle of Philippi. Horace had returned early but Pompeius stayed in the army longer. Too much attention has been paid to Horace throwing away his shield and describing himself as *paventem*. It was a literary tradition from Greek times that poets discarded their shields in battle and, since good soldiers seldom boast of their exploits, the *paventem* may be modest or humorous. Few would suggest that Horace was a born soldier but he probably acquitted himself as well as the next man.

A Roman banquet was usually held in the open-air dining-room beneath a trellis of roses or other climbing plants. The diners reclined on couches. They rubbed perfumed oil or ointment on their hair and wore a garland round their heads. The expression *sub rosa* (= privately) comes from diners exchanging confidences under the trelliswork of roses.

notes

1-2. o . . . deducte, the poem opens with three vocatives *deducte, Pompei, prime*. **1. tempus in ultimum**, *tempus* here means 'a moment of danger', so 'to the extreme of danger'. **3. Quiritem**, as a Roman citizen'; most of the beaten side at Philippi were allowed to retain their Roman citizenship. **6-7. morantem . . . diem . . . fregi**, 'I broke the (tedium of the) lagging day', *i.e.* made it pass more quickly. **7-8. capillos**, accusative of respect.

9-16. Horace speaks lightly of his own involvement in the battle (lines 9-10 and 13-14) but otherwise seriously. **11-12. minaces . . . mento**, some take this humorously, ' 'and fearsome warriors bit the dust', but this goes badly with *fracta virtus*. It is a copy of a Homeric phrase for the defeated.

13-14. another copy of Homer, here humorous; the gods rescued Homeric warriors in this way. **15-16.** metaphor from a stormy sea. *unda* = 'the tide of war'. *fretis aestuosis*, 'on its seething waters'.

(for vocabulary see p.59)

A Roman legionary

> ergo obligatam redde Iovi dapem,
> longaque fessum militia latus
>   depone sub lauru mea nec
20   parce cadis tibi destinatis.
>
> oblivioso levia Massico
> ciboria exple, funde capacibus
>   unguenta de conchis. quis udo
>   deproperare apio coronas
>
25 curatve myrto? quem Venus arbitrum
> dicet bibendi? non ego sanius
>   bacchabor Edonis: recepto
>   dulce mihi furere est amico.

moist/drunk

parsley

myrtle

notes continued

18. latus, since Romans did not sit but reclined at meals.
23. conchis, shells or shell-shaped containers were used to hold perfumes. **quis
. . . curat**, Horace impatiently addresses his house-slaves – 'whose job is it to
. . .?'.
25. -ve, 'or' goes with *apio* and *myrto*. **25-26. quem . . . bibendi**, one diner was
chosen as master of ceremonies; his main job was to decide how much water was
added to the wine. He was chosen by throwing dice; *Venus* was the highest
throw. **26. non . . . sanius**, 'not more sanely than', *i.e.* 'just as madly as'. **27.
Edonis**, a Thracian tribe; Thracians were noted for their wild revels. **28.
furere**, 'to be mad' = the colloquial 'to let my hair down'.

vocabulary

āēr, aeris (m.) *mist*
apium (2) *parsley*
bacchor (1) *to celebrate*
cadus (2) *wine-jar*
cibŏrium (2) *a large cup*
concha (1) *a shell*
dēpropero (1) *to make quickly*
lēvis (adj.) *polished*

mālobathrum (2) *ointment, oil*
mentum (2) *chin*
obligātus (adj.) *due, owed*
obliviŏsus (adj.) *bringing forgetfulness*
parmula (1) *a little shield*
reddo (3) *to render*
resorbeo (2) *to suck back*
solum (2) *earth, soil*

Venus teaching Cupid to shoot an arrow, from a gilt bronze mirror cover with incised design, fourth century B.C.; Louvre, Paris.

SECTION III

Love

To us love is either a Christian virtue or a sentimental attachment often leading to marriage. The attachment will involve physical attraction but is assumed to rise above this and include friendship, compatibility etc. For us the ideal marriage is based on love in its highest conception. To the Romans this would all have been incomprehensible. Their religion had no command to love one's fellow-man. Friends might be loved but enemies were usually to be injured if not destroyed. Sentiment was of no account in marriage. Marriages were arranged between families to promote social or economic or political ambitions. If the young couple happened to like one another, so much the better, but that had nothing to do with the arrangement of the marriage.

The upper-class Roman met two sorts of women who were quite separate from one another. There were girls from good families whom one might marry. Some of these might be promiscuous and indiscreet but most of them ended up as brides in a marriage of convenience. The other sort of girls were courtesans, usually Greek, whom one made love to but never thought of marrying. The coarser ones provided only sexual satisfaction but many were endowed with charm and musical or literary talents. With the latter, young Romans went through all the joys and tribulations of sentimental love.

Horace never married. He came from a humble family and found himself mixing with the mighty. At any rate it is doubtful if he was suited to the ties and responsibilities of married life. This does not mean he was uninterested in women. He clearly had a long list of girl-friends. Their Greek names – Chloe, Pyrrha, Cinara – place them in the courtesan class; but not all the girls with Greek names are necessarily courtesans: Licymnia in *Odes II* 12 was probably Terentia the wife of Maecenas to whom the poem is addressed. Horace clearly derives more than physical pleasure from the company of these women. He laughs at their jealousy or their sentimentality; he appreciates Lalage's sweet laughter and Chloe's skill on the lyre. But, as in everything, Horace does not go to extremes. Love is to be enjoyed, but not overdone. It is doubtful if he was deeply attached to any of his girl-friends, though he speaks with some feeling of his affair with Cinara (Poem 24 lines 3-4).

Horace's poems on love are sometimes compared unfavourably with those of Catullus to his lady-friend Lesbia. Certainly Horace's poems lack the fire and burning passion of those addressed to Lesbia. But two things should be remembered. Horace was writing of girls one might enjoy but would never marry; Catullus' infatuation was with an elegant society woman (the name Lesbia stands for Clodia) in his own social sphere. Secondly, Horace was 35 to 40 when he wrote the odes; Catullus burned himself out as a young lover and died at the age of thirty.

POEM 19 (I 23)
(Asclepiad System 4)

vitas hinnuleo me similis, Chloe, *greenness, immaturity*
quaerenti pavidam montibus aviis
    matrem non sine vano
        aurarum et siluae metu.

5   nam seu mobilibus veris inhorruit
adventus foliis, seu virides rubum
    dimovere lacertae,
        et corde et genibus tremit.

      atqui non ego te, tigris ut aspera
10   Gaetulusve leo, frangere persequor:
    tandem desine matrem
        tempestiva sequi viro.

In this charming little poem Horace teases a timid young courtesan. 'What are you scared of?' he asks. 'You're a big girl now. Stop running crying to your mother.' The picture in the second stanza of the little fawn whose long legs tremble as a breeze rustles the leaves or lizards dart among the bushes is particularly fascinating.

notes

4. siluae, three syllables = *silvae*.
5-6. 'the arrival of spring quivers in the leaves', *i.e.* the gentle breeze of spring makes the leaves rustle.
10. frangere, infinitive of purpose after *persequor*. **11. tandem**, implies 'this has gone on long enough; now stop it!' **12. viro**, 'man', not 'husband'; marriage was not Chloe's immediate destiny.

vocabulary

atqui *and yet*
āvius (adj.) *remote, untrodden*
frango (3) *to crush, subdue*
genu, -ūs (n.) *the knee*
hinnuleus (2) *a young deer, fawn*

inhorresco, -ere, -horrui *to quiver*
lacerta (1) *a lizard*
mōbilis (adj.) *rustling*
rubus (2) *bramble-bush*
tempestīvus (adj.) *of an age for* + dat.

perfectly simple
perfectly finished

POEM 20 (I 5)
(Asclepiad System 4)

quis multa gracilis te puer in rosa
perfusus liquidis urget odoribus
grato, Pyrrha, sub antro?
cui flavam religas comam,

Simple with your charms
"in simple elegance"

5   simplex munditiis? heu quotiens fidem
mutatosque deos flebit et aspera
nigris aequora ventis   *Sea metaphor*
emirabitur insolens,

ablative

qui nunc te fruitur credulus aureā,

lovely   10   qui semper vacuam, semper amabilem *(te before)*
sperat, nescius aurae   *Sea metaphor*
treacherous/fickle   fallacis. miseri, quibus

picture *non*

intemptata nites. me tabulā sacer   *abl. means*
me is the subject
of suspendisse votivā pariẹs indicat uvida
15   suspendisse potenti
vestimenta maris deo.

Neptune
or Venus

As Horace laughs at the youth besotted by the redhead Pyrrha,
the best description of the poem is that used of its leading lady,
simplex munditiis, i.e. straightforward, elegant, unostentatious.
Pyrrha is frank in expressing her emotions and elegantly made up.
So is the poem. It is full of phrases that are apparently simple and
yet must have taken ages to prune and polish (e.g. *multa in rosa,
emirabitur insolens, nescius aurae fallacis* and *intemptata nites*). The
comparison of the uncertainties of Pyrrha's favours to a sea-voyage
in treacherous weather is happily maintained (*aspera aequora,
aurae fallacis* and lines 13-16).

The poet asks Pyrrha (apparently an ex-girl-friend with whom
he had had a stormy affair), 'What slim youth is pressing his love
on you now in some pleasant rose-curtained love-nest? He's
having a marvellous time now and fondly imagines it'll go on like
that; he'll learn! He'll find that your moods can change as quickly
and as often as the weather. Thank God I've learned my lesson and
am now immune!'

The power of sexual attraction exercised by an elegant and passionate woman on an infatuated youth is here treated humorously. But such power is, of course, universal and this fact gives added credibility to the situation.

notes

1. multa . . . in rosa, take this with *grato sub antro* (line 3). It is not clear whether the 'cave' is a natural feature or an artificial rose-surrounded grotto. **2. perfusus**, the prefix gives humorous emphasis, 'soaked in', 'dripping with'; cf. *e-* in *emirabitur* (line 8).

9. credulus, believing everything you say. **aurea**, 'golden', 'priceless (in his eyes)'. **10-11 sperat**, supply *te fore* with this verb. **11. aurae**, the fickle breeze of Pyrrha's favour.

13. nites, Pyrrha shines, smiles, sparkles with all her provocative charm. **13-16.** rescued sailors dedicated their clothes to Neptune, often accompanied by a picture (*tabula*) of the event; here Horace has been rescued from the shipwreck of his affair with Pyrrha.

vocabulary

flāvus (adj.) *reddish-yellow*

fleo (2)(trans.) *to weep over*

insolens (adj.) *unaccustomed*

intemptātus (adj.) *untried*

munditiae (pl.) *charms, elegance*

religo (1) *to bind back*

ūvidus (adj.) *dripping wet*

vacuus (adj.) *available*

POEM 21 (III 9)
(Asclepiad System 2)

donec gratus eram tibi,
    nec quisquam potior bracchia candidae
cervici iuvenis dabat,
    Persarum vigui rege beatior.

ablative

5   donec non aliā magis
    arsisti, neque erat Lydia post Chloen,
gen. description
"more distinguished" multi Lydia nominis
    Rōmana vigui clarior Ilia.

    me nunc Thressa Chloe regit,
10   dulces docta modos et citharae sciens,
pro qua non metuam mori,
my darling, to survive me si parcent animae fata superstiti.

    me torret face mutua
    Thurini Calais filius Ornyti,
15   pro quo bis patiar mori,
    si parcent puero fata superstiti.

    quid si prisca redit Venus
    diductosque iugo cogit aeneo,
us now separated
with brazen yoke si flava excutitur Chloe
20   reiectaeque patet ianua Lydiae?

    quamquam sidere pulchrior
    ille est, tu levior cortice et improbo
quick-tempered iracundior Hadria,
    tecum vivere amem, tecum obeam libens.

amoebaean song.

    This delightful piece of cross-talk between two lovers – Lydia and an unnamed youth – contains all the conventional elements of lover's tiff and reconciliation. 'I've another girl now. She's marvellous. I'd die for her.' 'I'm mad about my new boy-friend.' 'What about us getting together again?' 'You're nasty and fickle and bad-tempered but still, dammit – I love you!' Apart from the charm and humour of the poem itself, it shows that, even though marriage was out of the question, long-lasting ties could be formed between upper-class youths and courtesans.

The poem uses much technical language of love, frequent in love elegy particularly: *ardeo* + *abl.* (line 6) = to be on fire for; *rego* (line 9) = to rule, to be queen of (my) heart; *anima* (line 12) = darling; *torreo* (line 13) = to scorch, burn up; *fax* (line 13) = the torch, the fire of love.

notes

2. potior, 'favoured', *i.e.* in preference to me. **candidae**, a white skin was admired in women; Roman beauties did *not* go in for sun-bathing.
6. Chloen, Chloe had superseded Lydia. **7. multi . . . nominis**, describes Lydia. **8. Ilia**, mother of Romulus (also called Rhea Silvia).
10. citharae sciens, 'having knowledge of the lyre', *i.e.* an accomplished player. **12. superstiti**, predicative 'spare my darling to survive me'.
14. Thurini, from Thurii, an originally Greek city in the toe of Italy. **15. bis**, Lydia always tries to go one better.
17. quid si, tentative 'what would you say if . . .'. **18. diductos**, the prefix *di-* or *dis-* always denotes separation or dissolution. Supply *nos* with *diductos*. **20. Lydiae**, genitive; her door is again open for him.
22. ille, = Calais. **23. Hadria**, another reference to the roughness of the Adriatic. **24. amem . . . obeam**, 'I would love to . . . I would die . . .'.

vocabulary

aēneus (adj.) *of bronze*	**improbus** (adj.) *unruly*
cōgo (3) *to bring together*	**levis** (adj.) *light, fickle*
cortex, -icis *cork*	**libens** (adj.) *willingly*
doctus (adj. + acc.) *skilled in*	**nōmen, -inis** (n.) *fame*
excutio, -ere *to shake off*	**Thressa** (f.) *Thracian (woman)*
	vigeo (2) *to thrive*

- Competitive element
- 2nd singer follows form & subject matter, but caps previous.
1 - ① Lydia caps lover's feelings & her own state of bliss
3 - ② Corresponding confessions of love
5 - ③ What if own love returns?
suggestion that the poet was responsible for their split
we get deep feeling at end

POEM 22 (I 25)
(Sapphic)

parcius iunctas quatiunt fenestras
iactibus crebris iuvenes protervi,
nec tibi somnos adimunt, amatque
    ianua limen,

5   quae prius multum facilis movebat
cardines. audis minus et minus iam:
'me tuo longas pereunte noctes,
    Lydia, dormis?'

invicem moechos anus arrogantes
10   flebis in solo levis angiportu,
Thracio bacchante magis sub inter-
    lunia vento,

cum tibi flagrans amor et libido,
quae solet matres furiare equorum,
15   saeviet circa iecur ulcerosum,
    non sine questu,

laeta quod pubes hedera virenti
gaudeat pulla magis atque myrto,
aridas frondes hiemis sodali
Consign to east wind 20   dedicet Hebro.

This unpleasant little poem is included to show that the relationship between young Roman and courtesan was not all smiles and kisses. It reminds us that even charming and talented beauties grow old and that then their attractions and their desirability grow less. Some thrifty women would have saved and invested against advancing years, others might find husbands from lower down the social ladder. But there would always be many, like Lydia of this ode, who imagined that their charms would always find them clients, who had saved nothing from the presents showered on them; and who came to a miserable end as ageing common prostitutes.

We don't know if this Lydia is a real person or if Horace invents her to show that in this field also one must exercise restraint and remember the inexorable approach of old age and death. If Horace is getting his own back on a real person, it shows that our poet, like all of us, had his nastier moments.

notes

1. parcius, comparative adverb 'more rarely'. **2.** iactibus, 'with throws', 'with things thrown'. **3.** amat ianua limen, 'the door loves the threshold', *i.e.* remains closed, does not open to admit clients.
6. audis, 'you hear (men crying) . . .'. **7. me tuo**, 'while I your darling . . .'.
9. invicem, 'in your turn', *i.e.* just as they used to weep at your haughtiness.
moechos, strictly 'adulterers', here of the courtesans's customers. **11.**
Thracio . . . vento, Thrace was considered a wild and wintry place; *cf. Hebro* (the Thracian river Hebrus) line 20. **sub interlunia**, 'at the new moon', which was said to affect the weather.
14. comparing Lydia to a mare on heat. **15. iecur ulcerosum**, 'ulcerated liver', the supposed seat of the passions – translate 'diseased mind'. **16. non sine questu . . . quod** (line 17) 'not without a complaint because' translate freely 'and you also complain that . . .'.
17-20. the ivy and myrtle (blondes and brunettes?) represent youth, the withered leaves old age. The order is *magis gaudeat hedera virenti atque pulla myrto*.
19. hiemis, with *sodali*.

vocabulary

angiportus (4) *a narrow street*
baccho (1) *to rage*
cardo, -inis (m.) *hinge*
furio (1) *to madden*
gaudeo (2)(+ abl.) *to take delight in*

hedera (1) *ivy*
levis (adj.) *cheap, unimportant*
myrtus (f.) *myrtle*
pūbes (f.) *youth, young people*
pullus (adj.) *dark-green*
saevio (4) *to rage*

POEM 23 (III 26)
(Alcaic)

vixi puellis nuper idoneus
et militavi non sine gloria:
    nunc arma defunctumque bello
      barbiton hic paries habebit,

5   laevum marinae qui Veneris latus
custodit. hic, hic ponite lucida
    funalia et vectes et arcus
      oppositis foribus minaces.

    o quae beatam diva tenes Cyprum et
10   Memphin carentem Sithonia nive,
    regina, sublimi flagello
      tange Chloen semel arrogantem.

[margin handwritten notes:]

contrast Chloe's chilly treatment of poet

Sombre note as though life is over but it is his love life that is over — in a temple of Venus

- Prayer to Venus: high solemn style

- amusing surprise: asks for one more chance with Chloe — reason for his retirement not relevant

- dedication of tools
- dedication asking for success } combined. Retirement is the last thing he wants

    This is mainly a conventional 'retirement' poem, written in a metre which is rather heavy for such slight material. When soldiers left the army, when gladiators quitted the arena, when sailors retired from the sea, they dedicated the accoutrements of their trade to the appropriate god, accompanied by a graceful ode. Here Horace represents himself as retiring from the lists of love and dedicates lyre, crowbars, torches, etc. to Venus. If this was one of the last odes written in Books I-III, Horace was then about 40 and was perhaps tired of the routine wooing of temperamental beauties. But the poem should probably be treated as a formal exercise.

It is only rescued from aridity by the gleam of humour in the last few lines: 'I have finished with love, Venus – but, just before I go, would you mind laying one crack of your whip on that snooty little bitch, Chloe?' Horace could not keep a conventionally straight face for very long! Poem 24 provides a much more serious approach to the same subject.

notes

1. puellis . . . idoneus, 'able to cope with girls'. **3. defunctum bello**, 'which has done with war'. **4. barbiton**, 'lyre', accusative of the Greek *barbitos*. **5. Veneris**, 'of (the temple of) Venus. **7-8.** the idea of Horace using these instruments to storm his lady-love's door is as conventional as it is absurd. **9.** take *diva* before *quae*, 'O goddess who . . . '. **10. Sithonia nive**, Sithonia in Northern Greece was considered a cold and wintry place.

vocabulary

flagellum (2) *whip*
funāle (n.) *wax-torch*
lūcidus (adj.) *bright*
marīnus (adj.) *sea-born*

minax, -ācis (adj. + dat.) *a threat to*
sublīmis (adj.) *uplifted*
teneo (2) *to hold, have power in*
vectis (m.) *a crowbar*

Horace(?) in middle age, from a marble relief fragment of the early first century A.D.; Museum of Fine Arts, Boston.

72

POEM 24 (IV 1)
(Asclepiad System 2)

intermissa, Venus, diu
    rursus bella moves? parce precor, precor.
non sum qualis eram bonae
    sub regno Cinarae. desine, dulcium
5   mater saeva Cupidinum,
    circa lustra decem flectere mollibus
iam durum imperiis: abi,
    quo blandae iuvenum te revocant preces.
tempestivius in domum
10   Pauli purpureis ales oloribus
comissabere Maximi,
    si torrere iecur quaeris idoneum:
namque et nobilis et decens
    et pro sollicitis non tacitus reis
15   et centum puer artium
    late signa feret militiae tuae,
et quandoque potentior
    largi muneribus riserit aemuli,
Albanos prope te lacus
20   ponet marmoream sub trabe citrea.

(*cont.*

about 50 years.

When Horace wrote the last ode in Book III (Poem 13) at the age of 42, he certainly regarded it as his farewell to lyric poetry. But we are told that 10 years later Augustus urged him, or ordered him to compose odes in which Drusus, Tiberius and the emperor himself were honoured (Book IV 4, 5, 14 and 15).

Horace opens the fourth book with this strangely mixed poem. He wants to explain his resumption of lyric by a sudden late middle-age onset of physical passion but he manages to work into it some complimentary references to a friend of Augustus, Paulus Fabius Maximus, a successful barrister, who was consul in 11 B.C., and died in A.D. 14 just before Augustus.

The emotion here is physical rather than sentimental. Venus is described, as in *Odes* I 19, as *mater saeva Cupidinum* (fierce mother of desires). The goddess is implored to use her powers on Paulus, a younger and more suitable victim. Then, in lines 29-40, Horace insists he has done with love but, even as he protests, he feels a powerful homosexual yearning for young Ligurinus. Homosexuality was one of Rome's many legacies from Greek literature. It is impossible to decide whether lines 29-40 are merely conventional or represent genuine Catullan-like passion. They certainly sound genuine but, if so, they offend the Golden Mean and they give as unpleasant a picture of an ageing profligate as Poem 22 does of an ageing prostitute.

Some argue that his unwilling slavery to love is an oblique way of saying he didn't want to write Book IV at all!

notes

2. bella moves, the idea of love as warfare is common, *cf.* line 16 below. **precor, precor,** repetition is used throughout the poem: *et* (lines 13-17), *illic* (lines 21 & 25), *nec* (lines 29-32), *cur* (lines 33 & 35), *iam* (line 38), *te* (lines 39-40). **4. sub regno,** the girl 'rules' her lover, *cf.* Poem 21 line 9. **desine,** the order is *desine flectere (me) iam durum* . . . **6. circa lustra decem,** 'about fifty years old'. **mollibus . . . imperiis,** *mollis* does not mean 'gentle' but rather 'seductive', 'amorous'. **9. tempestivius,** 'more appropriately'. **10. ales,** adjective – 'borne on wings (by)'. **oloribus,** swans drew the chariot of Venus. **12. torrere,** see Poem 21 line 13. **iecur,** see Poem 22 line 15. **17-18.** i.e. when he has triumphed over a rival. **17. potentior,** 'more powerful' in love's battle. **18. muneribus riserit,** 'has laughed to see the gifts . . . '. **19. Albanos prope . . . lacus,** where Paulus had a villa. **te . . . ponet,** 'will place (a statue of) you'. *(for vocabulary see p. 75)*

illic plurima naribus
   duces tura, lyraeque et Berecyntiae
delectabere tibiae
   mixtis carminibus non sine fistula;
25   illic bis pueri die
   numen cum teneris virginibus tuum
laudantes pede candido
   in morem Salium ter quatient humum.
nec me femina nec puer
30   iam nec spes animi credula mutui
nec certare iuvat mero
   nec vincire novis tempora floribus.
sed cur heu, Ligurine, cur
   manat rara meas lacrima per genas?
35   cur facunda parum decoro
   inter verba cadit lingua silentio?
nocturnis ego somniis
   iam captum teneo, iam volucrem sequor
te per gramina Martii
40   Campi, te per aquas, dure, volubiles.

whirling

notes continued

22. Berecyntiae, from Mt. Berecyntus in Phrygia where Cybele was worshipped to a flute accompaniment. **25. bis . . . die,** 'twice a day'. **28. in morem Salium** (= *Saliorum*), 'like the Salii', the dancing priests of Mars. **29-32. iuvat,** 'pleases' first with *femina, puer, spes* as subject; and then impersonal 'it pleases' with *certare* and *vincire.* **30. spes animi credula mutui,** a fine phrase 'the fond hope of a love returned'. **35-36.** his passion renders him speechless. **35. parum,** with *decoro silentio.* **decoro,** the 'o' is elided before *inter* and gives the effect of stumbling speech. **38. iam . . . iam,** 'at one moment . . . at another'. **captum,** supply *te.* **39-40.** Ligurinus has been exercising in the Campus Martius and then cooling off with a swim in the Tiber.

vocabulary

blandus (adj.) *persuasive, winning*
candidus (adj.) *gleaming*
citreus (adj.) *of cedar-wood*
cōmissor (1) *to go in procession*
decens (adj.) *handsome*
dūco (3) *to draw in, inhale*
dūrus (adj.) *hard-hearted, tough*
fistula (1) *shepherd's pipe*
gena (1) *the cheek*
intermissus (adj.) *suspended, broken off*

largus (adj.) *free-spending*
lustrum (2) *a 5-year period*  purification rite at end of census every 5 years.
māno (1) *to trickle*
nāris, -is (f.) *nostril*
olor, -ōris (m.) *swan*
quandoque *whenever*
reus (2) *accused person*
tempora (n. pl.) *temples*
trabs, trabis (f.) *roof*
tūs, tūris (n.) *incense*
volucer, -cris (adj.) *flying, speeding*

Head of a young woman, from an engraved carnelian gem of the first century B.C.; Ashmolean Museum, Oxford.

Part of a tenth century A.D. manuscript of Horace's *Odes*, giving the opening of *Odes* I 1 (*Maecenas atavis edite regibus*); Bibliothèque Nationale, Paris.

SECTION IV

The Countryside

Was Horace a town-lover who liked to relax occasionally in his Sabine farm or was he a countryman who came to the city and made good? There is some truth in both propositions. He did like people and he did stroll in the Via Sacra observing them. But he was born on a small farm and, in his most impressionable years, was steeped in country lore. He must have known the practical side of farming long before Maecenas gave him a small estate near Tibur (modern Tivoli), north-east of Rome. He would also have observed the countryside with a poet's eye for detail, as in Poem 6 lines 11-12 where the bustling stream runs on its zig-zag course, and in Poem 19 lines 5-8 where the spring breeze rustles through the leaves and lizards dart among the bushes.

The Romans seldom romanticised nature or made a mystery of it. Horace never sat down to write what we would call a 'nature' poem in the Wordsworthian sense. The four poems presented here are only partly about the countryside: Poems 25, 26, 28 are partly religious, while 27 could equally well have been included in Section II on friends. The Romans were a down-to-earth, practical race and thought more of the fertility of their flocks and fields than of the beauty of flowers and hills. When they did think about nature, they thought of the countryside as inhabited by gods and of the legends connected with them. So, just as love was Venus and not romance and the sea was Neptune rather than an 'awesome element', nature was Faunus and the Nymphs, Diana the Huntress or Bacchus the wine-god and his wild revellers. The background to the activities of these gods, the beauties of nature, were usually taken for granted. This does not mean that the beauties were not appreciated. The siting of Roman villas along the Bay of Naples and elsewhere is proof that they were.

POEM 25 (III 18)
(Sapphic)

Faune, Nympharum fugientum amator,
per meos fines et aprica rura
lenis incedas abeasque parvis
    aequus alumnis,

5   si tener pleno cadit haedus anno
larga nec desunt Veneris sodali
vina craterae, vetus ara multo
    fumat odore.

ludit herboso pecus omne campo,
10   cum tibi Nonae redeunt Decembres;
festus in pratis vacat otioso
    cum bove pagus;

inter audaces lupus errat agnos;
spargit agrestes tibi silva frondes;
15   gaudet invisam pepulisse fossor
    ter pede terram.

This ode is in the form of a hymn to Faunus, god of farmers and shepherds; cf. Poem 1, a formal hymn to Mercury. Faunus was identified with the Greek countryside god Pan and so is made to pursue the Nymphs (whose main occupation would seem to have

been running away from such amorous advances). Once again
Horace ends on a light note with the labourer stamping on the
hated earth which he must toil to dig.

notes

3. incedas abeasque, wishes – 'may you . . . , if . . . '.
5. pleno anno, 'at the full year', *i.e.* when your festival (5th December) has
come round. **6. Veneris sodali,** with *craterae.*
9. ludit, the animals are free to enjoy themselves as are their masters
(*vacat . . . pagus,* lines 11-12). **10. tibi,** 'for you', 'in your honour'.
14. the leaves fall late in Italy; here they cover the ground in honour of Faunus
(*tibi*). **15. ter pede terram,** the words contain an almost audible thud!

vocabulary

aequus (adj.) *favourable, kindly*
alumni (2. pl.) *young animals*
aprīcus (adj.) *sun-drenched*

cratēra (1) *wine-bowl*
haedus (2) *young goat*
largus (adj.) *in plenty, abundant*
pāgus (2) *villager*

POEM 26 (III 25)
(Asclepiad System 2)

quo me, Bacche, rapis tui
    plenum? quae nemora aut quos agor in specus,
velox mente nova? quibus
    antris egregii Caesaris audiar
5   aeternum meditans decus
    stellis inserere et consilio Iovis?
dicam insigne, recens, adhuc
    indictum ore alio. non secus in iugis
exsomnis stupet Euhias
10   Hebrum prospiciens et nive candidam
Thracen ac pede barbaro
    lustratam Rhodopen, ut mihi devio
ripas et vacuum nemus
    mirari libet. o Naiadum potens
15   Baccharumque valentium
    proceras manibus vertere fraxinos,
nil parvum aut humili modo,
    nil mortale loquar. dulce periculum est
o Lenaee, sequi deum
20   cingentem viridi tempora pampino.

This is a fine poem but a strange one. Basically it is a hymn to Bacchus and, as such, contains references to the orgiastic nature of that god's worship. His female devotees, the Bacchantes or Maenades, inspired by wine and religious fervour, roamed through woods and mountains by night shrieking and dancing to drum and flute, tearing animal or human victims to pieces and even uprooting trees with their bare hands.

Into this hymn is inserted Horace's intention to glorify and immortalise the deeds of Augustus. The two aims fit rather awkwardly together. Horace seems to mean that, to do justice to Augustus, he would need the inspiration of Bacchus and that, so aided, he intends to produce something unseen and unattempted before. It is possible that Augustus, inspirer of his people, is by implication identified with Bacchus, but this is uncertain.

The core of the poem is the comparison in lines 8-14. As Horace, in a fit of creative inspiration, sees in his mind's eye the untrodden poetic paths he will explore, he likens himself to a dazed Bacchante staring open-mouthed at the wild winter landscape. This sense of wonder at the vastness and beauty of nature is rare in classical literature.

notes

1. tui, genitive of *tu*. **2. specus**, the Bacchantes sometimes slept in caves and Bacchus himself was brought up in one: *cf. antris* (line 4). **3. velox mente nova**, 'swift with a new mind', *i.e.* my mind racing with original ideas. **quibus antris**, 'by what caves'; Horace imagines himself among the Bacchantes. **6.** referring to two separate honours: *stellis inserere* is to set Augustus as a new constellation in the sky; *consilio Iovis inserere* implies outright deification. **7. dicam**, 'I shall say something . . .'. **8. indictum ore alio**, *cf. Odes* III, I line 2 – *carmina non prius audita . . . canto*. **non secus**, followed by *ut* in line 12 – 'in just the same way as . . . so'. **10. prospiciens**, 'looking out over'. **11. pede barbaro lustratam**, 'traversed by her wild feet'. **12. Rhodopen**, Greek accusative of *Rhodope* (feminine), a mountain range in Thrace. **devio**, 'as I follow untrodden paths' **13. vacuum**, 'where no one goes', to be taken with both *ripas* and *nemus*. **16. vertere**, for *evertere*.

vocabulary

decus (n.) *glory*
Euhias (f.) *a Bacchante*
exsomnis (adj.) *unsleeping*
fraxinus (f.) *ash-tree*
Lēnaeus (2) *Bacchus*
lustro (1) *to traverse*
meditor (1) *to plan*

Nāïades (f. pl.) *water-nymphs*
pampinus (2) *a vine-leaf*
potens (adj. + gen.) *master of*
prōcērus (adj.) *tall*
rapio, -ere *to carry along*
specus (4) *a cave*
valens (adj.) *powerful enough to*

POEM 27 (II 6)
(Sapphic)

Septimi, Gades aditure mecum et
Cantabrum indoctum iuga ferre nostra et
barbaras Syrtes, ubi Maura semper
    aestuat unda:

5   Tibur Argeo positum colono
sit meae sedes utinam senectae,
sit modus lasso maris et viarum
    militiaeque.

unde si Parcae prohibent iniquae,
10   dulce pellitis ovibus Galaesi
flumen et regnata petam Laconi
    rura Phalantho.

ille terrarum mihi praeter omnes
angulus ridet, ubi non Hymetto
15   mella decedunt viridique certat
    baca Venafro,

ver ubi longum tepidasque praebet
Iuppiter brumas et amicus Aulon
fertili Baccho minimum Falernis
20   invidet uvis.

ille te mecum locus et beatae
postulant arces, ibi tu calentem
debita sparges lacrima favillam
    vatis amici.

This poem is much less complex than Poem 26. Horace says to his friend Septimius, 'I know you would go to the ends of the earth with me, but I would like to spend my last years at Tibur or, if that may not be, at Tarentum where you may shed a tear over the ashes of your poet-friend'.

The love of the countryside in lines 13-20, beginning with *ille terrarum mihi praeter omnes angulus ridet,* speaks for itself. There is a rather melancholy atmosphere of approaching old age and death. This may be a reaction after the crucial battle of Actium (31 B.C.). Lines 7-8 suggest that the poet may have seen service at that battle.

The poem contains a large number of proper names, which are listed below in alphabetical order with brief explanations:

Argeo: Argeus = Argive, from Argos in Greece.
Aulon: a valley near Tarentum in southern Italy.
Cantabrum: the Cantabri, a tribe in northern Spain.
Falernis: the *ager Falernus* in Campania produced excellent grapes.
Gades: Cadiz.
Galaesi: the river Galaesus, near Tarentum.
Hymetto: Mt. Hymettus near Athens, famous for its honey.
Laconi: Laconis = Spartan.
Maura: Maurus = Mauretanian, from the area of modern Morocco.
Phalantho: Phalanthus, the Spartan who founded Tarentum.
Syrtes: quicksands off the North African coast.
Venafro: Venafrum, noted for its olive-oil.

notes

2. **iuga ferre,** defeated enemies were compelled, as a sign of submission, to walk under an ox's yoke hanging from a tree. 5. **colono,** dative of agent after *positum.*
7. **modus,** 'limit (to toil)'. **lasso,** with gen. 'tired of', supply *mihi.*
10. **pellitis ovibus,** 'with its sheep clothed in skins', to protect their valuable wool. 12. **Phalantho,** dative of agent after *regnata* 'ruled over by'.
13. **mihi . . . ridet,** 'smiles for me', *i.e.* has a cheerful, pleasant atmosphere.
18. **amicus,** with *fertili Baccho,* 'friendly to'. 19. **minimum,** adverb – 'very little', 'not at all'.
21. **beatae arces,** probably 'fertile hills' near Tarentum rather than 'rich buildings' within it. 22. **postulant,** 'claim you', 'demand your presence'.

vocabulary

bāca (1) *the olive berry*
brūma (1) *winter*
calens (adj.) *warm*
certo (1) *to contend (with), to rival*
dēcēdo (3) *to yield to*
favilla (1) *ashes*

indoctus (adj.) *not taught (to)*
inīquus (adj.) *unfavourable*
Parcae (f. pl.) *Fates*
praeter (+ acc.) *beyond*
tepidus (adj.) *mild*
ūva (1) *a grape*

POEM 28 (III 13)
(Asclepiad System 4)

o fons Bandusiae splendidior vitro,
dulci digne mero non sine floribus,
    cras donaberis haedo,
        cui frons turgida cornibus

5   primis et venerem et proelia destinat;
frustra: nam gelidos inficiet tibi
    rubro sanguine rivos
        lascivi suboles gregis.

       te flagrantis atrox hora Caniculae
10   nescit tangere, tu frigus amabile
    fessis vomere tauris
        praebes et pecori vago.

       fies nobilium tu quoque fontium,
me dicente cavis impositam ilicem
15   saxis, unde loquaces
        lymphae desiliunt tuae.

This is one of the best-known of Horace's odes and as such it is often read superficially and without any appreciation of the layers of meaning in it. The outer layer is a formally religious one: streams and fountains have their spirits which require sacrifice; Horace selects a young goat as his victim. Next is the mock-heroic element: his little spring shall be exalted by his poetry to rival the Castalian spring at Delphi, Hippocrene on Mt. Helicon and Dirce near Thebes. (This in fact did happen; for the *fons Bandusiae* is now as well or better known than Castalia, Hippocrene or Dirce.)

Finally, the real picture painted by the poem is of an ever-flowing supply of sparkling water in a hot and thirsty Italian country side. From the little rocky grotto under the spreading oak-tree there bubbles up cold life-giving water. As the summer sun beats down pitilessly, the cattle slake their thirst and find shelter in the shade beside the babbling stream.

notes

1. Bandusiae, whether the fountain was on Horace's Sabine farm or near his birthplace Venusia is of no importance for an appreciation of the poem. **4. cui,** translate as genitive, 'whose forehead . . . '.

6. frustra, Horace is fond of this emphatic position for such adverbs (*cf.* Poem 12, lines 13 & 15. **tibi,** 'in your honour'.

9. Caniculae, the Dog-Star or Sirius, whose rising ushered in the blazing (*flagrantis*) summer heat. Horace's use of repeated *te . . . tu . . . tu* binds the poem together, as often in prayers (*cf.* Poem 1, note on line 17).

13. nobilium . . . fontium, '(one) of the famous fountains'. **14. me dicente,** 'as I tell of' – the object is *ilicem.* **16. tuae,** not a weak ending; it means *yours* as opposed to the waters of Castalia, etc.

vocabulary

destino (1) *to foretell*
dōno (1) *to present*
infĭcio, -ere *to stain*
loquax, -ācis (adj.) *babbling*
nēscio (4) *to be unable*

splendidus (adj.) *bright, clear*
suboles (f.) *offspring*
turgidus (adj.) *swelling*
vitrum (2) *glass, crystal*

Silver *denarius* of Augustus, struck about 20 B.C.; British Museum, London.

SECTION V

The Roman State

The following account of Horace's attitude to the State is partly conjectural but the conjectures do not seem to go against any positive evidence. (See also Introduction, *Life of Horace*.)

Horace was of humble country stock and certainly had no knowledge of, or connection with the ruling classes. He owed his education to the energies and determination of his father. It is probable that, if he thought of politics at all, he supported the republican system under which Rome had risen to greatness. In 43 B.C. he was studying at Athens and, with other students, received with enthusiasm the news of the death of Julius Caesar. When Brutus and Cassius reached Greece, they were hailed by the young Romans as liberators. Horace may have travelled with Brutus to Asia Minor. He was certainly enrolled as a tribune in Brutus' army and fought at the batle of Philippi in 42 B.C.

After the defeat of Brutus, Horace's enthusiasm waned. He did not join those who wished to continue the struggle to restore the republic. Already he showed a dislike of going to extremes. He returned to Italy under the amnesty and fell on lean times during the years 42-39 B.C. His property had been confiscated and he had to take a job as a clerk in the Treasury. One of his earliest poems shows that he was deeply pessimistic at this time. He was tired of civil strife and thought how good it would be to leave Rome and find some blessed land where one could live in peace.

His condition changed for the better when he was received into Maecenas' literary set in 38 B.C. but even then he was not fully convinced that Octavian (the future Augustus) deserved unqualified support. He would remember that Octavian had supported the political murders of 43 B.C. and had acquiesced in the death of Cicero. The first book of the *Satires,* published about 33-32 B.C., contains no complimentary references to Octavian.

The moment for decision came in 32 B.C. when Octavian and Antony split. There was now no possibility of a restoration of the old republican constitution. One had to choose between Octavian and Antony as future ruler of Rome's destiny. Antony's liaison with Cleopatra and the thought of an Egyptian queen lording it on the Capitol decided Horace and thousands of others in favour of Octavian. It is possible that Horace fought at the battle of Actium in 31 B.C.

From then on it must have been clear to Horace that Augustus (as he was now called) was the one hope for a peaceful and rejuvenated Italy. The poet's relations with the emperor grew steadily in warmth until, by the end of his life, he regarded Augustus as a friend rather than an employer.

Horace can be described as a court poet but he was never at all interested in day-to-day politics. Indeed he refused a secretaryship offered him by Augustus. In the first three books of the *Odes* he is seldom comfortable when directly praising Augustus and his policies. Even the so-called 'Roman' odes or 'state' poems that introduce Book III deal much more with social and philosophical matters than with current politics; and Poem 29 (I 37), which starts with joy at the Actium victory, changes to a description of the death of Cleopatra. Book IV which was commissioned by Augustus is the nearest Horace comes to flattery of the imperial house (e.g. IV 4, 5, 14 and 15). One gets the impression that

Horace was interested in the spiritual revival of Italy but that his heart was not in the role of poet laureate.

*　　*　　*　　*　　*

Gold *aureus* of M. Antonius (Antony), struck in 40 B.C. when Antony married Octavian's (Augustus') sister Octavia, whom he deserted for Cleopatra; Berlin.

90

POEM 29 (I 37)

(Alcaic)

nunc est bibendum, nunc pede libero
pulsanda tellus, nunc Saliaribus
   ornare pulvinar deorum
      tempus erat dapibus, sodales.

5   antehac nefas depromere Caecubum
cellis avitis, dum Capitolio
   regina dementes ruinas
      funus et imperio parabat

contaminato cum grege turpium
10   morbo virorum, quidlibet impotens
   sperare fortunaque dulci
      ebria sed minuit furorem

vix una sospes navis ab ignibus
mentemque lymphatam Mareotico
15   redegit in veros timores
      Caesar, ab Italia volantem

remis adurgens, accipiter velut
molles columbas, aut leporem citus
   venator in campis nivalis
20   Haemoniae, daret ut catenis

(cont.

This poem, oddly enough, improves as it gets away from its main purpose – congratulations to Octavian on the victory over Antony and Cleopatra at Actium. The first few stanzas, apart from the exultant rhythm of the first line and a half, are pedestrian. It is when Horace comes to describe the brave death of Cleopatra that the verse becomes poetry. Her death is doubtless meant to increase the victor's glory but in fact it leaves us sympathetic to the queen. A devoted court poet would perhaps never have allowed that to happen.

There is some historical inaccuracy and telescoping. Despite line 13, Cleopatra's ships all escaped from Actium and, despite lines 16 to 21, Octavian did not follow her to Egypt until the next year (30 B.C.).

notes

1. libero, double meaning 'unrestrained' and 'unconquered'. **2. Saliaribus**, *Saliaris*, adjective from *Salii* (see Poem 24 line 28 note); feasts connected with priests were notoriously lavish. **3. pulvinar**, a couch for displaying images of the gods at a thanksgiving.

5. antehac, scanned here as a dissyllable. **8. et**, to be taken before *funus*.

9. the order is *cum contaminato grege virorum turpium morbo* (foul with disease); the 'men' are Cleopatra's Egyptian eunuchs. **10-12. impotens . . . ebria**, agreeing with *regina*; *sperare* is epexegetic (explanatory) infinitive – 'carried away so as to hope for . . . '.

15. redegit, 'brought her mind . . . to a state of genuine fear' as distinct from the mad hopes of lines 10-12. **16.** supply *eam* with *volantem*.

(*for vocabulary see p.93*)

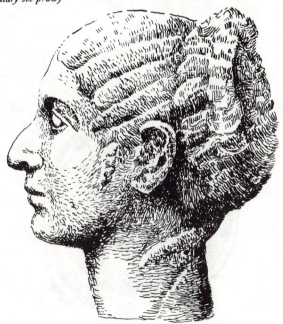

Cleopatra(?), a Greek portrait head of about 40 B.C.; British Museum, London (no. 1873). (For a less flattering portrait, see p.93.)

fatale monstrum: quae generosius
perire quaerens nec muliebriter
expavit ensem nec latentes
    classe cita reparavit oras.

25 ausa et iacentem visere regiam
vultu sereno, fortis et asperas
tractare serpentes, ut atrum
    corpore combiberet venenum,

deliberata morte ferocior,
30 saevis Liburnis scilicet invidens
privata deduci superbo
    non humilis mulier triumpho.

[handwritten marginalia: invective; elaborate structure power + precision; "royal city prostrate in defeat"; determined; even; and; poem of triumph ends with Roman word]

Reverse of silver *denarius* of Augustus, showing Venus as victor, bearing the inscription of CAESAR DIVI F(ilius) referring to Augustus, struck soon after 31 B.C.; British Museum, London.

notes continued

21. quae, feminine because the *monstrum* is Cleopatra. **23. nec . . . reparavit oras**, 'nor did she seek in exchange (for Egypt) some secret shores', *i.e.* she didn't abandon Egypt.

25-32. this long sentence, with its many nominatives describing Cleopatra, must be broken up in translation. **25. iacentem**, 'humbled by defeat'. **26. fortis**, with *tractare* – 'brave enough to handle'.

29. i.e. she was fiercer when death had been decided on than she had been in the battle. **30. Liburnis**, the light vessels of Octavian's fleet. **30-32.** very hard to translate; take *deduci* with *invidens* 'envying of course the fierce Liburnian ships (the glory of) having her led as a private citizen in a proud triumph – for she was a proud woman herself.'

vocabulary

accipiter (m.) *a hawk*
adurgeo (2) *to follow closely*
āter (adj.) *deadly*
avītus (adj.) *ancestral*
Caecubum (2) *Caecuban wine*
cella (1) *store-room*
expavesco, -ere, -pāvi *to dread*
fātālis (adj.) *deadly*
fūnus (n.) *ruin*

generōsus (adj.) *noble*
Haemonia (1) *Thessaly*
lepus, -oris (m.) *a hare*
lymphātus (adj.) *raving mad*
Mareōticum (2) *Egyptian wine*
muliēbriter (adv.) *in womanly fashion*
nivālis (adj.) *snowy*
viso (3) *to look at*

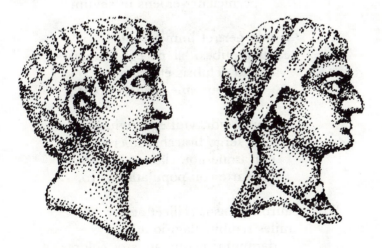

Antony and Cleopatra, from the obverse and reverse of a silver *denarius* struck in 32 B.C., the year before Actium; British Museum, London.

POEM 30 (III 5)
(Alcaic)

caelo tonantem credidimus Iovem
regnare: praesens divus habebitur
    Augustus adiectis Britannis
        imperio gravibusque Persis.

5   milesne Crassi coniuge barbara
    turpis maritus vixit, et hostium –
        pro curia inversique mores! –
           consenuit socerorum in armis

        sub rege Medo Marsus et Apulus,
10   anciliorum et nominis et togae
        oblitus aeternaeque Vestae,
           incolumi Iove et urbe Roma?

        hoc caverat mens provida Reguli
    dissentientis condicionibus
15   foedis et exemplo trahentis *trahenti*
           perniciem veniens in aevum,

        si non periret immiserabilis
    captiva pubes. 'signa ego Punicis
        adfixa delubris et arma
20   militibus sine caede,' dixit,

        'derepta vidi; vidi ego civium
    retorta tergo bracchia libero,
        portasque non clausas et arva
           Marte coli populata nostro.

25   auro repensus scilicet acrior
    miles redibit. flagitio additis
        damnum: neque amissos colores
           lana refert medicata fuco,

                          (cont.

53 BC?

cdapts an old phrase |

The first six odes of Book III in Alcaic metre are usually called 'the Roman odes' but they are 'state' poems in only a limited sense. Their purpose is not to explain or commend laws dealing with everyday government but rather to support the vaguer, but equally important side of Augustus' programme, the restoration of the old Roman way of life which had been corroded by increased wealth, contact with foreigners and the bitter civil wars. So III 1, preaching moderation, supports laws against luxury but in a philosophical manner and without any mention of the laws themselves; III 6 (Poem 3) urges the rebuilding of temples and moral reform; III 2 (Poem 5), a hymn to *virtus*, seeks to inculcate Stoic principles.

III 5 is placed in this section because it is a 'state' poem in the widest and deepest sense. An eloquent hymn to courage, it is clearly meant to support the policy of a return to the beliefs that made Rome great. The verses on Regulus are one of the high spots in Latin literature. Horace is carried away by Regulus as he was by Cleopatra in Poem 29 (I 37).

After a brief eulogy of Augustus, Horace deplores the conduct of the soldiers captured by the Parthians after the defeat of Crassus in 53 B.C. They had forgotten that Romans die rather than come to terms with an unconquered enemy. He then tells the story of Regulus who insisted on this principle. He was captured by the Carthaginians in North Africa in 255 B.C. along with thousands of his men. He was given parole to return to Rome and negotiate peace terms. He urged the Senate not to make peace and not to ransom the prisoners. He then returned to Africa where he died.

notes

1-3. we have (always) believed that Jupiter the Thunderer ruled in the heavens: Augustus will be considered a god on earth (*praesens* – 'present' – contrasted with *caelo*, though the word also carries the sense of a 'propitious' deity) when he has . . .; the deification of Augustus is put in the *future*.

5-12. a very long interrogative sentence *milesne Crassi . . . vixit . . . et consenuit Marsus et Apulus . . . oblitus* (with four genitives). **7. pro**, a dramatic exclamation, 'oh, to think of . . .'. **8. in armis**, in the ranks of', 'serving as allies of'.

9. Marsus et Apulus, 'Marsian and Apulian', two Italian peoples.

13. hoc caverat, 'had taken precautions against this', *i.e.* against condoning such behaviour in Roman troops. **15. exemplo**, 'by such a precedent'.

20. sine caede, 'without a struggle'.

22. retorta tergo bracchia, 'their arms twisted behind their backs'. **libero**, translate with *civium*, 'though they were free Romans'. **24. Marte . . . nostro**, 'by our warfare' *i.e.* by our soldiers.

25. scilicet, 'I suppose', ironical.

(*for vocabulary see p. 97*)

nec vera virtus, cum semel excidit,
30   curat reponi deterioribus.
si pugnat extricata densis
   cerva plagis, erit ille fortis,

qui perfidis se credidit hostibus,
et Marte Poenos proteret altero,
35   qui lora restrictis lacertis
   sensit iners timuitque mortem.

hic, unde vitam sumeret inscius,
pacem duello miscuit. o pudor!
o magna Carthago probrosis
40   altior Italiae ruinis!'

fertur pudicae coniugis osculum
parvosque natos ut capitis minor
ab se removisse et virilem
   torvus humi posuisse vultum,

(deminutio capitis — technical phrase)

45   donec labantes consilio patres
firmaret auctor nunquam alias dato,
interque maerentes amicos
   egregius properaret exsul.

atqui sciebat quae sibi barbarus
50   tortor pararet; non aliter tamen
dimovit obstantes propinquos
   et populum reditus morantem,

quam si clientum longa negotia
diiudicata lite relinqueret,
55   tendens Venafranos in agros
   aut Lacedaemonium Tarentum.

notes continued

30. curat reponi deterioribus, 'cares to be replaced in inferior bodies'. **31. si pugnat**, 'if (a doe) fights' as, of course, it does not.

38. pacem duello miscuit, 'mixed peace with war' – the ultimate disgrace; no Roman soldier should think of peace while the enemy was unconquered.

40. altior, 'raised higher' on Italy's ruin.

41-43. fertur . . . ab se removisse, 'he is said to have pushed away from him'. **42. ut capitis minor**, 'as one deprived of full citizen rights', *i.e.* by allowing himself to be captured. **44. posuisse**, 'to have set', 'to have turned'.

45. donec, (he kept looking at the ground) 'until he should confirm'. **consilio . . . dato**, 'by such advice as was never given at any other time'. **48. egregius exsul**, oxymoron (the combination of two contradictory terms in one phrase).

49. atqui, see Poem 19 line 9. **50. non aliter**, translate with *quam si* (line 53), 'exactly as if . . .'.

53. longa, 'long drawn-out', 'tedious'. **54. diiudicata lite**, 'the law-suit having been settled'. **55-56.** as he pictures a man leaving for a country holiday, Horace relieves the reader's feelings by letting the emotional tension ease. The place-names are chosen for their sound. For Horace's love of Tarentum, cf. Poem 27.

vocabulary

ancilium (2) *a sacred shield*
cerva (1) *a doe*
consenesco, -ere, -senui *to grow old*
cūria (1) *senate-house*
dīmoveo, -ēre, -mōvi *to move aside*
dissentio (4) *to disagree with*
fūcus (2) *purple (dye)*
gravis (adj.) *troublesome*
immiserābilis (adj.) *unpitied*
iners (adj.) *gutless* without acting
inversus (adj.) *perverted*

labo (1) *to waver*
lōra (n.pl.) *thongs*
medico (1) *to dye*
plaga (1) *a net*
populo (1) *to lay waste*
probrōsus (adj.) *shameful*
prōtero (3) *to trample down*
pūbes (f.) *youth, young people*
refero *to regain*
repensus (adj.) *ransomed*
tortor (m.) *torturer*
torvus (adj.) *grim*

POEM 31 (III 14)
(Sapphic)

Herculis ritu modo dictus, o plebs,
morte venalem petiisse laurum,
Caesar Hispana repetit Penates
    victor ab ora.

5   unico gaudens mulier marito
prodeat iustis operata sacris
et soror clari ducis et decorae
    supplice vitta

virginum matres iuvenumque nuper
10   sospitum. vos, o pueri et puellae
non virum expertae, male ominatis
    parcite verbis.

hic dies vere mihi festus atras
eximet curas: ego nec tumultum,
15   nec mori per vim metuam tenente
    Caesare terras.

i, pete unguentum, puer, et coronas,
et cadum Marsi memorem duelli,
Spartacum si qua potuit vagantem
20   fallere testa.

dic et argutae properet Neaerae
murreum nodo cohibere crinem;
si per invisum mora ianitorem
    fiet, abito.

25   lenit albescens animos capillus
litium et rixae cupidos protervae;
non ego hoc ferrem calidus iuventa
    consule Planco.

This ode exemplifies perfectly Horace's attitude to a state occasion. Augustus has returned safely from Spain in 24 B.C. The first three stanzas are rigid and formal. The fourth a linking verse, states that Horace has confidence in Augustus' leadership. Then, in the last three stanzas, the poet turns with obvious relief to preparations for his own celebrations. The ending, with its touch of wry humour, is very distant from the atmosphere of the opening stanzas.

notes

1. Herculis ritu, 'after the manner of Hercules'. **modo dictus**, 'recently reported to have sought . . .'. **2. morte venalem**, 'to be bought by death'; Augustus was seriously ill in Spain.

6. iustis operata sacris, 'having sacrificed with due offerings'. **8. supplice vitta**, 'with wreath of wool in thanksgiving'.

11. read *non* for manuscript *iam*. **male ominatis**, 'ill-omened'.

13. vere, with *festus*.

17. puer, 'slave'. **18. Marsi . . . duelli**, *i.e.* laid down 91-88 B.C. during the Marsian or Social War. **19. Spartacum**, Spartacus led the slave insurrection of 73-71 B.C. **si qua**, 'if by any means'.

21. properet, supply *ut*. **24. abito**, 'go away' *i.e.* don't argue with him.

26. cupidos, '(previously) eager for . . .'. **28. consule Planco**, *i.e.* in 42 B.C. when Horace was 23 years of age.

vocabulary

argūtus (adj.) *clear-voiced*	**protervus** (adj.) *vulgar, violent*
calidus (adj.) *hot-headed*	**rixa** (1) *a fight*
lēnio (4) *to make gentle*	**tumultus** (4) *civil war*
lītes (f.pl.) *quarrels*	**ūnicus** (adj.) *unparalleled*
murreus (adj.) *brown*	

POEM 32 (IV 5)
(Asclepiad System 3)

divis orte bonis, optime Romulae
custos gentis, abes iam nimium diu;
maturum reditum pollicitus patrum
    sancto concilio, redi.

5   lucem redde tuae, dux bone, patriae:
instar veris enim vultus ubi tuus
adfulsit populo, gratior it dies
    et soles melius nitent.

ut mater iuvenem, quem Notus invido
10   flatu Carpathii trans maris aequora
cunctantem spatio longius annuo
    dulci distinet a domo,

votis ominibusque et precibus vocat,
curvo nec faciem litore dimovet:
15   sic desideriis icta fidelibus
    quaerit patria Caesarem.

tutus bos etenim rura perambulat,
nutrit rura Ceres almaque Faustitas,
pacatum volitant par mare navitae,
20   culpari metuit Fides,

(cont.

Augustus has been compaigning in Gaul. Horace begs him to return. His country yearns for him as does a mother for her sailor son. It should be recalled that Book IV was commissioned by Augustus about 10 years after Books I-III. In it Horace is much more obviously the court poet. Throughout this poem Augustus is kept to the forefront, not mentioned briefly before being replaced by philosophy or history or mythology or, as in Poem 31 (III 14), by the poet's own feelings.

Though Augustus had deserved well of his country and though what Horace says here of the peace that reigns in Italy is true, there is still to be felt in this poem the intrusion of flattery unnoticed in *Odes* I-III (see e.g. lines 5-8). Whether he believed it or not, Horace now accepts the emperor as at least a demi-god, in the same category as Castor or Hercules.

notes

1. divis orte bonis, 'sprung from kindly gods'; cf. Poem 33 lines 31-32, where Augustus' divine pedigree is again alluded to. **Romulae**, here an adjective. **3. patrum . . . concilio**, 'to the council of the fathers', *i.e.* to the Senate.
6. instar veris, 'like spring'; Augustus' face makes the sun shine brighter!
9. ut mater iuvenem, the verbs with *mater* are *vocat* (line 13) and *dimovet* (line 14). **invido flatu**, 'with jealous breath'; it envies her the happiness of seeing her son. **10. Carpathii**, the Carpathian sea lies east of Crete. **11. spatio longius annuo**, he has not been able to return before winter ended the sailing season.
13. ominibus, 'by consulting omens'.
17. etenim, 'for (while Augustus is in charge of things) . . .'. **19. pacatum**, *i.e.* free from pirates. **20. culpari metuit Fides**, 'one's word of honour fears to be questioned', *i.e.* men make sure that their word is their bond.

(for vocabulary see p. 103)

nullis polluitur casta domus stupris,
mos et lex maculosum edomuit nefas,
laudantur simili prole puerperae,
    culpam poena premit comes.

25   quis Parthum paveat, quis gelidum Scythen,
quis Germania quos horrida parturit
fetus, incolumi Caesare? quis ferae
    bellum curet Hiberiae?

condit quisque diem collibus in suis,
30   et vitem viduas ducit ad arbores;
hinc ad vina redit laetus et alteris
    te mensis adhibet deum;

te multa prece, te prosequitur mero
defuso pateris, et Laribus tuum
35   miscet numen, uti Graecia Castoris
    et magni memor Herculis.

'longas o utinam, dux bone, ferias
praestes Hesperiae!' dicimus integro
sicci mane die, dicimus uvidi,
40   cum sol Oceano subest.

notes continued

23. simili, either 'like their husbands' and so legitimate or 'as good as their fathers'. **24. poena . . . comes**, 'punishment that follows close on the crime'
25. gelidum Scythen, 'the Scythian from frozen Russia'. **26.** the order is *quis (paveat) fetus quos Germania . . . parturit . . .?*
29. condit . . . diem, 'stores away the day', 'sees the day end'. **30. vitem viduas**, vines were trained around tree-trunks, usually elms; the tree is *vidua* before it is so embraced! **31. hinc**, 'from here', 'from work'. **alteris mensis**, 'at the second course', *i.e.* when the household gods were toasted.
34. Laribus . . . numen, 'joins your godhead with that of his Lares'; the Lares were household guardian spirits. **35. uti**, = *ut*, 'just as'.
39. sicci . . . uvidi, 'before we have drunk anything . . . mellow with wine'.
40. for the quiet ending again, *cf.* Poem 30.

vocabulary

adhibeo (2) *to call upon, summon*
cūro (1) *to worry about*
ēdomo, -āre, -ui *to subdue completely*
Faustitas (f.) *Prosperity*
fēriae (f.pl.) *holidays, festivals*
fidēlis (adj.) *loyal*
Hesperia (1) *Italy*
horridus (adj.) *rough, shaggy*
maculōsus (adj.) *stained, defiled*
patera (1) *a dish*
polluo (3) *to pollute*
premo (3) *to suppress, restrict*
prōsequor (3) *to honour*
puerpera (1) *a woman with child*
stuprum (2) *adultery*
viduus (adj.) *unwed*

POEM 33 (IV 15)
(Alcaic)

Phoebus volentem proelia me loqui
victas et urbes increpuit lyra,
    ne parva Tyrrhenum per aequor
      vela darem. tua, Caesar, aetas

5   fruges et agris rettulit uberes,
et signa nostro restituit Iovi
    derepta Parthorum superbis
      postibus, et vacuum duellis

    Ianum Quirini clausit et ordinem
10   rectum evaganti frena licentiae
    iniecit emovitque culpas
      et veteres revocavit artes,

    per quas Latinum nomen et Italae
crevere vires famaque et imperi
15   porrecta maiestas ad ortus
      solis ab Hesperio cubili.

(cont.

Augustus and his achievements are celebrated throughout this, the last of Horace's odes. There is a catalogue of many of the items from other 'state' odes – revival of agriculture, purity of home life, rebirth of the qualities that made Rome great. But the main theme is the *Pax Romana*, the closing of the Temple of Janus and the fact that no civil war, no foreign enemy could disturb the quiet of Italy.

The verse is as competent as ever but enthusiasm is lacking. The change of subject in line 4 is most abrupt. Horace is going through the motions capably and willingly but without any fire or depth or excitement. He has said it all before. He is a true friend and supporter of Augustus but it is contrary to his nature to express this in formal encomiums and hymns of praise. The old idea of 'Let's have a party to celebrate' is now confined to one line *inter iocosi munera Liberi*.

So Horace, who wrote his first odes when taken up by Maecenas in an Italy whose future was still uncertain, ends his career as a lyric poet by extolling Augustus who seems to have solved all the problems. We pass from Odes I 1.1 *Maecenas atavis edite regibus* to Odes IV 15.31-2 where Augustus is *almae progeniem Veneris*.

notes

1. me . . . increpuit lyra, 'made a noise with his lyre at me', 'warned me off with a note on his lyre'. **3-4.** not to cross the wide ocean in my little boat, *i.e.* not to attempt mighty subjects with my slender Muse. **vela dare**, 'to spread sails'.

6. signa, the standards lost at Carrhae; see Poem 30 line 5. **nostro Iovi**, 'to our (temple of) Juppiter (on the Capitol). **8. vacuum duellis**, 'free from wars'.

9. Ianum, a *ianus* was a gateway with two doors; it was lucky to enter by one and go out by the other. Armies setting off must march out by the lucky door. The closing of the *Ianus Quirini* (Romulus' Gateway) meant there were no more wars to march out to. **ordinem rectum**, 'the right path'.

14. imperi, = *imperii*, 'of the empire'. **15. porrecta** *(est)*, 'has been extended'. **16. ab Hesperio cubili**, 'from his bed in the West', where the sun rested after his journey across the heavens.

(for vocabulary see p. 107)

custode rerum Caesare non furor
civilis aut vis exiget otium,
   non ira, quae procudit enses
20   et miseras inimicat urbes.

non qui profundum Danuvium bibunt
edicta rumpent Iulia, non Getae,
   non Seres infidive Persae,
     non Tanain prope flumen orti.

25   nosque et profestis lucibus et sacris
inter iocosi munera Liberi,
   cum prole matronisque nostris
     rite deos prius adprecati,

virtute functos more patrum duces
30   Lydis remixto carmine tibiis
   Troiamque et Anchisen et almae
     progeniem Veneris canemus.

notes continued

21-24. the peoples mentioned are those living by the Danube (*Danuvium*), Thracians (*Getae*), dwellers in the East (*Seres*), Parthians (*Persae*), Russians (born near the River Tanais, the modern Don). **22. edicta . . . Iulia**, 'the orders of Augustus'.

25. profestis lucibus, 'on non-feast days'. **26.** 'as we enjoy the gifts of cheerful Bacchus (*Liberi*)'.

29. virtute functos, 'who have performed courage', *i.e.* who have lived (and died) courageously. **more patrum**, with *canemus*. **30. remixto**, 'alternating with'. **31-32.** we shall sing Rome's story from Troy and Anchises up to their descendant Augustus (*progeniem Veneris*); Aeneas was the son of Venus and Anchises. His son Iulus (Ascanius) was regarded as the founder of the Julian family.

vocabulary

ēvagor (1) *to wander from*
exigo (3) *to drive out*
inicio (+ acc. & dat.) *to lay (something) on*
inimīco (1) *to set at variance*

Lȳdus (adj.) *Lydian*
prōcūdo (3) *to forge, hammer out*
prōgenies (5) *descendant*
rīte (adv.) *duly, properly*
tībia (1) *pipe, flute*
ūber, -eris (adj.) *abundant*

CONCLUSION

One who was no friend of Horace could describe him as ' a fat little hedonist with a knack for writing verse'. This three-fold verdict requires consideration.

Horace, though dark and handsome in youth, did put on weight and did become prematurely grey. He describes himself at age 44 as *corporis exigui, praecanum, solibus aptum* (not very tall, prematurely grey, fond of sunshine). Suetonius in his *Life of Horace* calls him *brevis et obesus* (short and plump). So the first part of the description is found to be correct.

A hedonist? There is no doubt that Horace liked the pleasures of life and shunned anything that laid undue responsibility on him. He refused the offer of a secretaryship in the imperial civil service. His fondness for the pleasures of love is clear from Poems 19, 23 and 24 and his almost automatic reaction to good news or the arrival of a friend is to lay on a big party with plenty of wine and music and laughter (Poems 9, 16, 17, 18, 29 and 31). So the second part of the description is true.

Not even Horace's worst enemy would deny his verse-writing ability. The whole description is, therefore, true; but it is not the whole truth. There are three factors not taken into account in this facile character sketch.

Horace had a sanity of outlook and an instinct for moderation that raised him above the level of the shallow pleasure seeker. In Poem 7 (*rectius vives, Licini* . . .) he states his creed and he seldom departs from it. He had the ability to stand outside things and take a humorous look at the world. He could laugh at intense lovers (Poem 21), he could laugh at himself in love (Poem 23), he could even laugh at philosophy when it became too pompous. It was this moderation which prevented him from becoming a cog in the imperial propaganda machine. He could praise Augustus for his gift of peace to Italy but he could not descend into the depths of flattery found, for example, in Ovid. He could thank Maecenas for favours received but could politely excuse himself from joining his patron in Rome during the sickly season. He loved leisure and comfort but not to the extent of sacrificing his independence.

There was another side to Horace beside the Epicurean love of pleasure. He had a deep respect and love for his father who had ensured that he had the best education available (see *Satires* I. 6. 65-89). In his affection for his friends he allowed no moderation (Poem 15). He must not be thought of as a smart townee. His delight in his Sabine farm and in the countryside generally is often expressed (*e.g.* Poem 28). His support of Augustus' campaign to revive the old Roman virtues is wholehearted; see *e.g.* the Regulus ode (Poem 30) or such lines as these from Poem 3

> *non his iuventus orta parentibus*
> *infecit aequor sanguine Punico.*

Horace had much more than a 'knack for writing verse'. He had studied at Athens, was well read in the Greek lyric poets and fulfilled his burning ambition to adapt their metres to the Latin language. He has an exalted awareness of his great calling. He is *vates, Musarum sacerdos* and can claim *exegi monumentum aere perennius* (Poem 13). He has no great originality of thought but his method of expressing ordinary ideas – the sound, the rhythm, the choice of words – are exquisite (see *e.g.* Poem 12). He has his frigid banal moments like the beginning of Poem 31 but it was no mere versifier who

wrote Poem 6 or the end of Poem 30 or the last lines of
Poem 10:

dum loquimur, fugerit invida
aetas: carpe diem, quam minimum credula postero.

In summary, one can do no better than T. E. Page in
his introduction to the *Odes* and *Epodes*:

The man who wrote of his father as Horace did of his was not a bad
man; the man who amid all the temptations of Rome could make a
simple country life his ideal, as Horace did, was not a vicious man;
the man who kept his head in a position such as Horace occupied
was not a vain man; the man whom Augustus asked to be his
private secretary was not a foolish man; and there must have been
something very lovable and very remarkable in one whom
Maecenas, after an unbroken intimacy of 30 years, could
commend to his master on his death-bed with the words – *Horati
Flacci ut mei memor esto* (remember Horace as you will myself).

FURTHER READING

After careful reading of the thirty-three poems included in this volume and critical questioning of the views expressed, it may be helpful to continue as follows:

1. For a fuller knowledge of Horace and his work:
   L. P. Wilkinson: *Horace and his Lyric Poetry* (Cambridge U.P., 1945).
   G. Williams: *The Nature of Roman Poetry* (Oxford U.P., 1970).

2. For further reading in the *Odes:*
   T. E. Page: *Horace, Odes and Epodes* (Macmillan, 1890) – text with notes – replaced but not superseded by **K. Quinn:** *Horace, Odes* (Macmillan, 1981).
   H. E. Gould & J. L. Whiteley: *Horace, Odes I* (Macmillan, 1952) – text with notes and vocabulary.
   G. Williams: *Horace, Odes III* (Oxford U.P., 1969).
   R. G. M. Nisbet & M. Hubbard: *A Commentary on Horace Odes Book I* (Oxford U.P., 1970) ; *A Commentary on Horace Odes Book II* (Oxford U.P., 1978) – commentary only but extremely detailed.

3. For further study of Horace in rather more specialized works:
   E. Fraenkel: *Horace* (Oxford U.P., 1957).
   G. Williams: *Tradition and Originality in Roman Poetry* (Oxford U.P., 1968) – a fuller version of *The Nature of Roman Poetry* (see 1 above).
   D. West: *Reading Horace* (Edinburgh U.P., 1967).
   C. D. N. Costa (ed.): *Essays on Horace* (Routledge/Kegan Paul, 1973).
   J. K. Newman: *Augustus and the New Poetry* (Collection Latomus: Leiden, 1967).
   S. Commager: *The Odes of Horace: a Critical Study* (Yale U.P., 1962).

4. For reading in Horace's other works and study of them:
   O. A. W. Dilke: *Horace, Epistles I* (Methuen, 1961) – with vocabulary.
   A. Palmer: *Horace, Satires* (Macmillan, 1883).
   J. Gow: *Horace, Satires I* (Cambridge, Pitt Press, 1901).

   M. J. McGann: *Studies in Horace Epistles I* (Collection Latomus 100: Leiden 1969).
   N. Rudd: *The Satires of Horace* (Cambridge U.P., 1966)

INDEX OF FIRST LINES
(Poem numbers in brackets)